PENGUIN PARALLEL TEXTS

GERMAN SHORT STORIES · 1

GERMAN SHORT STORIES · 1
DEUTSCHE KURZGESCHICHTEN · 1

Edited by Richard Newnham

PENGUIN BOOKS

PENGUIN BOOKS

Published by the Penguin Group
Penguin Books Ltd, 80 Strand, London WC2R 0RL, England
Penguin Putnam Inc., 375 Hudson Street, New York, New York 10014, USA
Penguin Books Australia Ltd, 250 Camberwell Road, Camberwell, Victoria 3124, Australia
Penguin Books Canada Ltd, 10 Alcorn Avenue, Toronto, Ontario, Canada M4V 3B2
Penguin Books India (P) Ltd, 11 Community Centre, Panchsheel Park, New Delhi – 110 017, India
Penguin Books (NZ) Ltd, Cnr Rosedale and Airborne Roads, Albany, Auckland, New Zealand
Penguin Books (South Africa) (Pty) Ltd, 24 Sturdee Avenue, Rosebank 2196, South Africa

Penguin Books Ltd, Registered Offices: 80 Strand, London WC2R 0RL, England

www.penguin.com

First published 1964
20

Copyright © Penguin Books Ltd, 1964
All rights reserved

Printed in England by Clays Ltd, St Ives plc
Set in Monotype Bembo

CONTENTS

INTRODUCTION

THIS volume of German stories presents eight of the outstanding post-war authors who write or are published in West Germany (two of them are Austrian). No attempt has been made to represent modern writing in all German-speaking countries, nor to draw regional or political distinctions between the literatures of the two Germanies, Austria, and Switzerland, since this would be beyond the scope of a book of so few pages.

Parallel texts are set out primarily with the student in mind. If he has worked conscientiously through grammar and exercises and now wants something more satisfying than processed gobbets, these stories may be just what he needs. Non-linguists, reading the English versions alone, may detect something of the flavour of modern German literature, a sharp and largely bitter one that dates from the end of the Second World War. The stories have been printed in approximate order of difficulty.

★

The situation of the German writer during the first months of peace may be compared with that of the returned soldier in Heinrich Böll's story printed here. Back in his home town he knows no one, has nothing to say, and has few words left that are not linked to painful memories. For more than twelve years German literature had been, if not itself politically tainted, then at best a witness to taint. After the black-listing presidential decree of February 1933, the burning of the books, and

the suppression of Jewish authors and publishers, many writers had emigrated either in the literal sense to Switzerland, America, or Moscow, or else had made an 'inner emigration'. Those who continued to write and be published were faced with compromise even on language. As well as perverting thought, Hitler's hacks perverted German prose, a good example being the Führer's own attack (ironically, on 'decadent' writers) in his speech at the opening of the Haus der Deutschen Kunst – a crescendo of repetitions in loan-words and non-words, quite un-German in tone.

The returned writer, then, found an audience too poor to buy books and too sceptical to have much faith in the written word. An official 'rehabilitation of literature' began, but small credit for results is due to the Allied Occupation. The morbid fear of Nazi ghosts, coupled with some remarkably *ad hoc* exorcism, the censorship, and indeed the whole concept of democratization, struck the young writers (many of them like Borchert openly anti-Fascist) as just another cliché. They knew how easily a refuge from responsibility lay behind such words. Something more was needed. The year 1947 saw the adoption of what has become known as the *Kahlschlag* ('clean sweep') policy: a return to honesty of language, based on popular non-literary usage, and to honesty of theme, based on personal experience. 'Policy' is perhaps too solid and formal a word; the centre of this movement, the Gruppe 47, in fact began as (and has since remained) an informal seminar whose aims have never been openly declared and whose members carry no cards. The group was started after the U.S. military government had closed a periodical that had found fault with the Occupation and its attempts at re-education. Since then its influence has been wide; at least three of the present

authors have attended its sessions, and the danger that an intellectual élite would become a clique seems to have been avoided.

For many of these writers, the most attractive form has been the short story. The reason for this preference may be that the *Kurzgeschichte* has no literary pedigree in Germany, and indeed is viewed with mistrust by many critics who favour the more didactic *Novelle* with its respectable antecedents in nineteenth-century literature. Previously, works shorter than the *Novelle* had been classed either as *Anekdoten* (dramatic episodes of a narrative kind – one thinks of authors such as Grimmelshausen, Kleist, J. P. Hebel, and Wilhelm Schäfer) or as *Skizzen* (generally plot-less studies in atmosphere: the Swiss Robert Walser wrote many such). The short story is not quite either form, and an uneasy debate on its German possibilities had begun in the twenties and thirties ('are we soon to have the *Langgeschichte*?' asked one theoretician). But in 1945 it seemed perfectly to match the post-war mood of irony, objectivity, and mistrust of the didactic. By an accident, it was the Occupation's best gift to German culture; Bender has written:

It exactly hit off the only mood left to us after the war. Following the catastrophe, German literature *had* to make a fresh start with the short story. Furthermore, our conquerors brought it with them. In the first books and magazines issued under licence were American and English short stories. . . .

Imitations, particularly of Hemingway's staccato style, were soon followed by new wine in new bottles. What the German writers have made of their new form can be judged, it is hoped, from the variety of this selection. GAISER and FUSSENEGGER both explore the world of

private obsession, one whimsically, the other warningly (the love of self-destruction is not limited to Germany). LETTAU and SCHNURRE are satirists, with very different targets. BORCHERT and AICHINGER experiment with form and language while keeping their intelligibility and humanity. BÖLL and BENDER, against the same post-war landscape, write of the resumption of life by two quite dissimilar heroes who share the same sense of isolation.

*

Acknowledgements are due to the following German, Swiss, and British publishers for permission to include German originals or new English translations in this book: for Heinrich Böll to Paul List Verlag, Munich; for Ilse Aichinger to S. Fischer Verlag, Frankfurt am Main, and Secker and Warburg Ltd; for Hans Bender, Gerd Gaiser, and Reinhard Lettau to Carl Hanser Verlag, Munich; for Wolfdietrich Schnurre to Walter Verlag, Olten; for Wolfgang Borchert to Rowohlt Verlag, Hamburg.

RICHARD NEWNHAM

PALE ANNA

HEINRICH BÖLL

Translated by Christopher Middleton

DIE BLASSE ANNA

ERST im Frühjahr 1950 kehrte ich aus dem Krieg heim, und ich fand niemanden mehr in der Stadt, den ich kannte. Zum Glück hatten meine Eltern mir Geld hinterlassen. Ich mietete ein Zimmer in der Stadt, dort lag ich auf dem Bett, rauchte und wartete und wußte nicht, worauf ich wartete. Arbeiten zu gehen, hatte ich keine Lust. Ich gab meiner Wirtin Geld, und sie kaufte alles für mich und bereitete mir das Essen. Jedesmal, wenn sie mir den Kaffee oder das Essen ins Zimmer brachte, blieb sie länger, als mir lieb war. Ihr Sohn war in einem Ort gefallen, der Kalinowka hieß, und wenn sie eingetreten war, setzte sie das Tablett auf den Tisch und kam in die dämmrige Ecke, wo mein Bett stand. Dort döste ich vor mich hin,[1] drückte die Zigaretten an der Wand aus, und so war die Wand hinter meinem Bett voller[2] schwarzer Flecken. Meine Wirtin war blaß und mager, und wenn im Dämmer ihr Gesicht über meinem Bett stehen blieb, hatte ich Angst vor ihr. Zuerst dachte ich, sie sei verrückt, denn ihre Augen waren sehr hell und groß, und immer wieder fragte sie mich nach ihrem Sohn. «Sind Sie sicher, daß Sie ihn nicht gekannt haben? Der Ort hieß Kalinowka – sind Sie dort nicht gewesen?»

Aber ich hatte nie von einem Ort gehört, der Kalinowka hieß, und jedesmal drehte ich mich zur Wand und sagte: «Nein, wirklich nicht, ich kann mich nicht entsinnen.»

Meine Wirtin war nicht verrückt, sie war eine sehr ordentliche Frau, und es tat mir weh, wenn sie mich fragte. Sie fragte mich sehr oft, jeden Tag ein paarmal,

PALE ANNA

It wasn't until spring 1950 that I came back from the war, and I found there was nobody I knew left in the town. Luckily my parents had left me some money. I rented a room in the town, lay there on the bed, smoked and waited, and didn't know what I was waiting for. I didn't want to work. I gave my landlady money and she bought me everything and cooked my food. Every time she brought coffee or a meal to my room, she stayed there longer than I liked. Her son had been killed at a place called Kalinovka, and when she had come in she would put the tray on the table and come over to the dim corner where my bed stood. There I dozed and vegetated, stubbed the cigarettes out against the wall, and so all over the wall by my bed there were black marks. My landlady was pale and thin, and when her face paused over my bed in the half-light, I was afraid of her. At first I thought she was mad, for her eyes were very bright and large, and again and again she asked me about her son. 'Are you certain you didn't know him? The place was called Kalinovka – didn't you ever go there?'

But I'd never heard of a place called Kalinovka, and each time I turned to the wall and said: 'No, really I didn't, I can't remember.'

My landlady wasn't mad, she was a very decent woman, and it hurt me when she asked me. She asked me very often, several times a day, and if I went to her in the kitchen I had to look at her son's picture, a

und wenn ich zu ihr in die Küche ging, mußte ich das Bild ihres Sohnes betrachten, ein Buntphoto, das über dem Sofa hing. Er war ein lachender blonder Junge gewesen, und auf dem Buntphoto trug er eine Infanterie-Ausgehuniform.

«Es ist in der Garnison gemacht worden,» sagte meine Wirtin, «bevor sie ausrückten.»

Es war ein Brustbild: er trug den Stahlhelm, und hinter ihm war deutlich die Attrappe einer Schloßruine zu sehen, die von künstlichen Reben umrankt war.[3]

«Er war Schaffner,» sagte meine Wirtin, «bei der Straßenbahn. Ein fleißiger Junge.» Und dann nahm sie jedesmal den Karton voll Photographien, der auf ihrem Nähtisch zwischen Flicklappen und Garnknäueln stand. Und ich mußte sehr viele Bilder ihres Sohnes in die Hand nehmen: Gruppenaufnahmen aus der Schule, wo jedesmal vorne einer mit einer Schiefertafel zwischen den Knien in der Mitte saß, und auf der Schiefertafel stand eine VI, eine VII, zuletzt eine VIII.[4] Gesondert, von einem roten Gummiband zusammengehalten, lagen die Kommunionbilder: ein lächelndes Kind in einem frackartigen schwarzen Anzug, mit einer Riesenkerze in der Hand, so stand er vor einem Transparent, das mit einem goldenen Kelch bemalt war. Dann kamen Bilder, die ihn als Schlosserlehrling vor einer Drehbank zeigten, das Gesicht rußig, die Hände um eine Feile geklammert.

«Das war nichts für ihn,» sagte meine Wirtin, «es war zu schwer.» Und sie zeigte mir das letzte Bild von ihm, bevor er Soldat wurde: er stand in der Uniform eines Straßenbahnschaffners neben einem Wagen der Linie 9 an der Endstation, wo die Bahn ums Rondell kurvt, und ich erkannte die Limonadenbude, an der ich so oft Zigaretten gekauft hatte, als noch kein Krieg war; ich erkannte die Pappeln, die heute noch dort stehen, sah die Villa mit den goldenen Löwen vorm Portal, die heute nicht mehr

coloured photograph which hung over the sofa. He'd been a laughing, fair-haired boy, and in the coloured photograph he wore an infantryman's walking-out uniform.

'It was taken at the barracks,' my landlady said, 'before they went to the front.'

It was a half-length portrait: he wore a steel helmet, and behind him you could see quite distinctly a dummy ruined castle, with artificial creepers all over it.

'He was a conductor,' my landlady said, 'in a tram. A hard-working boy.' And then she took, each time, the box of photographs which stood on her sewing-table between patches and tangles of thread. And always she pressed lots of pictures of her son into my hands: school groups, on each of which one boy sat in the middle of the front row with a slate between his knees, and on the slate there was a 6, a 7, finally an 8. In a separate bundle, held together by a red rubber band, were the Communion pictures: a smiling child in a black suit like a dress suit, with a giant candle in his hand, that was how he stood, in front of a diaphane on which a gold chalice was painted. Then came pictures which showed him as a locksmith's apprentice at a lathe, with smudges on his face and his hands gripping a file.

'That wasn't the job for him,' my landlady said, 'the work was too heavy.' And she showed me the last picture of him, before he became a soldier: there he stood, in a tram-conductor's uniform, beside a number 9 tram at the terminus, where the tracks curve round the circle, and I recognized the refreshment stand at which I'd so often bought cigarettes, when there had still been no war; I recognized the poplars, which are still there today, saw the villa with the golden lions at the gate,

dort stehen, und mir fiel das Mädchen ein, an das ich während des Krieges oft gedacht hatte: sie war hübsch gewesen, blaß, mit schmalen Augen, und an der End-station der Linie 9 war sie immer in die Bahn gestiegen.

Jedesmal blickte ich sehr lange auf das Photo, das den Sohn meiner Wirtin an der Endstation der 9 zeigte, und ich dachte an vieles: an das Mädchen und an die Seifen-fabrik, in der ich damals gearbeitet hatte, ich hörte das Kreischen der Bahn, sah die rote Limonade, die ich im Sommer an der Bude getrunken hatte, grüne Zigaretten-plakate und wieder das Mädchen.

«Vielleicht», sagte meine Wirtin, «haben Sie ihn doch gekannt.»

Ich schüttelte den Kopf und legte das Photo in den Karton zurück: es war ein Glanzphoto und sah noch neu aus, obwohl es schon acht Jahre alt war.

«Nein, nein,» sagte ich, «auch Kalinowka – wirklich nicht.»

Ich mußte oft zu ihr in die Küche, und sie kam oft in mein Zimmer, und den ganzen Tag dachte ich an das, was ich vergessen wollte: an den Krieg, und ich warf die Asche meiner Zigarette hinters Bett, drückte die Glut an der Wand aus.

Manchmal, wenn ich abends dort lag, hörte ich im Zimmer nebenan die Schritte eines Mädchens, oder ich hörte den Jugoslawen, der im Zimmer neben der Küche wohnte, hörte ihn fluchend den Lichtschalter suchen, bevor er in sein Zimmer ging.

Erst als ich drei Wochen dort wohnte, als ich das Bild von Karl wohl zum fünfzigsten Mal in die Hand genom-men,[5] sah ich, daß der Straßenbahnwagen, vor dem er lachend mit seiner Geldtasche stand, nicht leer war. Zum ersten Mal blickte ich aufmerksam auf das Photo und sah, daß ein lächelndes Mädchen im Inneren des Wagens

which aren't there any more, and I remembered the girl whom I'd often thought of during the war: she'd been pretty, pale, with slit eyes, and she'd always boarded the tram at the number 9 terminus.

Each time I would have a long look at the photo which showed my landlady's son at the number 9 terminus, and I thought of a lot of things: of the girl and of the soap factory where I used to work in those days; I heard the tram's screeching, saw the red lemonade which I drank at the stand in the summer, green cigarette advertisements, and again the girl.

'Perhaps', my landlady said, 'you knew him after all.'

I shook my head and put the photo back into the box: it was a glossy photo and still looked new, though it was eight years old.

'No, no,' I said, 'Kalinovka too, really I didn't.'

I had to go to her in the kitchen often, and she often came to my room, and all day I was thinking of what I wanted to forget: the war – and I flicked my cigarette ash off behind the bed, stubbed out the butt against the wall.

Sometimes as I lay there in the evening I heard a girl's footsteps in the next room, or I heard the Jugoslav who lived in the room beside the kitchen, heard him cursing as he hunted for the light switch before going into his room.

It wasn't until I'd been there three weeks and had taken Karl's picture into my hands for about the fiftieth time, that I saw that the tram-car, in front of which he was standing with his satchel, smiling, wasn't empty. For the first time I looked attentively at the photo, and saw that a smiling girl inside the car had got into the

17

mitgeknipst worden war. Es war die Hübsche, an die ich
während des Krieges so oft gedacht hatte. Die Wirtin kam
auf mich zu, blickte mir aufmerksam ins Gesicht und sagte:
«Nun erkennen Sie ihn, wie?» Dann trat sie hinter mich,
blickte über meine Schulter auf das Bild, und aus ihrer
zusammengerafften Schürze stieg der Geruch frischer
Erbsen an meinem Rücken herauf.

«Nein,» sagte ich leise, «aber das Mädchen.»

«Das Mädchen?» sagte sie, «das war seine Braut, aber
vielleicht ist es gut, daß er sie nicht mehr sah – »

«Warum?» fragte ich.

Sie antwortete mir nicht, ging von mir weg, setzte sich
auf ihren Stuhl ans Fenster und hülste weiter Erbsen aus.
Ohne mich anzusehen, sagte sie: «Kannten Sie das
Mädchen?»

Ich hielt das Photo fest in meiner Hand, blickte meine
Wirtin an und erzählte ihr von der Seifenfabrik, von der
Endstation der 9 und dem hübschen Mädchen, das dort
immer eingestiegen war.

«Sonst nichts?»

«Nein,» sagte ich, und sie ließ die Erbsen in ein Sieb
rollen, drehte den Wasserhahn auf, und ich sah nur ihren
schmalen Rücken.

«Wenn Sie sie wiedersehen, werden Sie begreifen,
warum es gut ist, daß er sie nicht mehr sah – »

«Wiedersehen?» sagte ich.

Sie trocknete ihre Hände an der Schürze ab, kam auf
mich zu und nahm mir vorsichtig das Photo aus der
Hand. Ihr Gesicht schien noch schmäler geworden zu
sein, ihre Augen sahen an mir vorbei, aber sie legte leise
ihre Hand auf meinen linken Arm. «Sie wohnt im Zimmer
neben Ihnen, die Anna. Wir sagen immer blasse Anna zu
ihr, weil sie so ein weißes Gesicht hat. Haben Sie sie
wirklich noch nicht gesehen?»

picture. It was the pretty girl whom I'd often thought of during the war. The landlady came over, looked attentively into my face and said: 'Now do you know him, do you?' Then she went behind me and from her tucked-in apron the smell of fresh green peas came up over my back.

'No,' I said quietly, 'but I do know the girl.'

'The girl?' she said. 'She was his fiancée, but perhaps it's a good thing he never saw her again –'

'Why?' I asked.

She didn't answer, walked away from me, sat down on the chair by the window and went on shelling peas. Without looking at me she said: 'Did you know the girl?'

I held the photo firmly in my hand, looked at my landlady and told her about the soap factory, about the number 9 terminus and the pretty girl who always boarded the tram there.

'Nothing else?'

'No,' I said, and she let the peas roll into a sieve, turned on the tap, and I saw only her narrow back.

'When you see her again, you'll realize why it's good he saw no more of her –'

'See her again?' I said.

She dried her hands on her apron, came up to me, and carefully took the photo out of my hand. Her face seemed even thinner now, her eyes looked past me, but she gently put her hand on my left arm. 'She lives in the room next to yours, Anna does. We always call her pale Anna, because she has such a white face. Haven't you really seen her yet?'

«Nein», sagte ich, «ich habe sie noch nicht gesehen, wohl ein paarmal gehört. Was ist denn mit ihr?»

«Ich sag's nicht gern, aber es ist besser, Sie wissen es. Ihr Gesicht ist ganz zerstört, voller Narben – sie wurde vom Luftdruck in ein Schaufenster geschleudert. Sie werden sie nicht wiedererkennen.»

Am Abend wartete ich lange, bis ich Schritte in der Diele hörte, aber beim ersten Male täuschte ich mich: es war der lange Jugoslawe, der mich erstaunt ansah, als ich so plötzlich in die Diele stürzte. Ich sagte verlegen «Guten Abend» und ging in mein Zimmer zurück.

Ich versuchte, mir ihr Gesicht mit Narben vorzustellen, aber es gelang mir nicht, und immer, wenn ich es sah, war es ein schönes Gesicht auch mit Narben. Ich dachte an die Seifenfabrik, an meine Eltern und an ein anderes Mädchen, mit dem ich damals oft ausgegangen war. Sie hieß Elisabeth, ließ sich aber Mutz nennen, und wenn ich sie küßte, lachte sie immer, und ich kam mir blöde vor. Aus dem Krieg hatte ich ihr Postkarten geschrieben, und sie schickte mir Päckchen mit selbstgebackenen Plätzchen, die immer zerbröselt[6] ankamen, sie schickte mir Zigaretten und Zeitungen, und in einem ihrer Briefe stand: «Ihr werdet schon siegen, und ich bin so stolz, daß du dabei[7] bist.»

Ich aber war gar nicht stolz, daß ich dabei war, und als ich Urlaub bekam, schrieb ich ihr nichts davon und ging mit der Tochter eines Zigarettenhändlers aus, der in unserem Haus wohnte. Ich gab der Tochter des Zigarettenhändlers Seife, die ich von meiner Firma bekam, und sie gab mir Zigaretten, und wir gingen zusammen ins Kino, gingen tanzen, und einmal, als ihre Eltern weg waren, nahm sie mich mit auf ihr Zimmer, und ich drängte sie im Dunkeln auf die Couch; aber als ich mich über sie beugte, knipste sie das Licht an, lächelte listig zu

20

'No,' I said, 'I haven't seen her yet, but I've heard her a few times. What's the matter with her?'

'I don't like to talk about it, but it's better if you know. Her face is completely ruined, scars all over it – she was thrown by the blast through a shop window. You won't recognize her.'

That evening I waited a long time, until I heard steps on the landing, but I was wrong the first time: it was the tall Jugoslav, and he looked at me in amazement as I rushed out so suddenly on to the landing. I said embarrassedly, 'Good evening,' and went back into my room.

I tried to imagine her face with scars, but I couldn't, and always when I saw it, it was a beautiful face even with scars. I thought of the soap factory, of my parents and of another girl whom I often went out with in those days. Her name was Elisabeth, but she let me call her Mutz, and whenever I kissed her she laughed and I felt silly. I'd written her postcards from the front, and she sent me little parcels with home-baked biscuits in them, which always arrived broken to pieces, she sent me cigarettes and newspapers, and in one of her letters she wrote: 'You lads will win, and I'm so proud that you're out there.'

But I wasn't at all proud to be out there, and when I got leave I didn't write to her about it, and went out with the daughter of a tobacconist who lived in our house. I gave the tobacconist's daughter soap that I got from my firm, and she gave me cigarettes, and we went to the cinema, went dancing, and once, when her parents were away, she took me to her room and in the dark I pushed her on to the couch; but as I bent over her she switched the light on, smiled craftily up at me, and in the glare I saw Hitler hung on the wall, a coloured

mir hinauf, und ich sah im grellen Licht den Hitler an der Wand hängen, ein Buntphoto, und rings um den Hitler herum, an der rosenfarbenen Tapete, waren in Form eines Herzens Männer mit harten Gesichtern aufgehängt, Postkarten mit Reißnägeln befestigt, Männer, die Stahlhelme trugen und alle aus der Illustrierten ausgeschnitten waren. Ich ließ das Mädchen auf der Couch liegen, steckte mir eine Zigarette an und ging hinaus. Später schrieben beide Mädchen mir Postkarten in den Krieg, auf denen stand, ich hätte mich schlecht benommen, aber ich antwortete ihnen nicht. . . .

Ich wartete lange auf Anna, rauchte viele Zigaretten im Dunkeln, dachte an vieles, und als der Schlüssel ins Schloß gesteckt wurde, war ich zu bange, aufzustehen und ihr Gesicht zu sehen. Ich hörte, wie sie ihr Zimmer aufschloß, drinnen leise trällernd hin und her ging, und später stand ich auf und wartete in der Diele. Sehr plötzlich war es still in ihrem Zimmer, sie ging nicht mehr hin und her, sang auch nicht mehr, und ich hatte Angst anzuklopfen. Ich hörte den langen Jugoslawen, der leise murmelnd in seinem Zimmer auf und ab ging, hörte das Brodeln des Wassers in der Küche meiner Wirtin. In Annas Zimmer aber blieb es still, und durch die offene Tür des meinen sah ich die schwarzen Flecke von den vielen ausgedrückten Zigaretten an der Tapete.

Der lange Jugoslawe hatte sich aufs Bett gelegt, ich hörte seine Schritte nicht mehr, hörte ihn nur noch murmeln, und der Wasserkessel in der Küche meiner Wirtin brodelte nicht mehr, und ich hörte das blecherne Rappeln, als die Wirtin den Deckel auf ihre Kaffeekanne schob. In Annas Zimmer war es immer noch still, und mir fiel ein, daß sie mir später alles erzählen würde, was sie gedacht hatte, als ich draußen vor der Tür stand, und sie erzählte mir später alles.

photograph, and all around Hitler, on the rose-coloured wallpaper, there were men with hard faces hanging, in the shape of a heart, postcards pinned up with tintacks, men who were wearing steel helmets and had all been cut out of the picture paper. I left the girl lying on the couch, lit a cigarette and walked out. Later, both girls sent me postcards at the front, in which they said that I'd behaved badly, but I didn't answer them. . . .

I waited a long time for Anna, smoked a lot of cigarettes in the darkness, thought of many things, and when the key was put into the lock, I was too scared to stand up and see her face. I heard her open her door, humming softly as she walked to and fro in her room, and later I got up and waited on the landing. Very suddenly it was quiet in her room, she wasn't walking to and fro any more, wasn't singing any more, and I was afraid to knock. I heard the tall Jugoslav murmuring softly and walking up and down in his room, heard the water boiling in my landlady's kitchen. But in Anna's room it was quiet, and through the open door of mine I saw on the wallpaper the black marks of the many cigarettes that I'd stubbed out.

The tall Jugoslav had lain down on his bed. I couldn't hear his footsteps any more, only heard him murmuring, and the kettle in my landlady's kitchen wasn't boiling any more, and I heard the metallic sound as the landlady clapped the lid on her coffee pot. In Anna's room it was still quiet, and it occurred to me that she would later tell me all the things she'd been thinking about as I'd stood outside her door, and later she did tell me everything.

Ich starrte auf ein Bild, das neben dem Türrahmen hing: ein silbrig schimmernder See, aus dem eine Nixe mit nassem blondem Haar auftauchte, um einem Bauernjungen zuzulächeln, der zwischen sehr grünem Gebüsch verborgen stand. Ich konnte die linke Brust der Nixe halb sehen, und ihr Hals war sehr weiß und um ein wenig zu lang.

Ich weiß nicht wann, aber später legte ich meine Hand auf die Klinke, und noch bevor ich die Klinke herunterdrückte und die Tür langsam aufschob, wußte ich, daß ich Anna gewonnen hatte: ihr Gesicht war ganz mit bläulich schimmernden kleinen Narben bedeckt, ein Geruch von Pilzen, die in der Pfanne schmorten, kam aus ihrem Zimmer, und ich schob die Tür ganz auf, legte meine Hand auf Annas Schulter und versuchte zu lächeln.

I stared at the picture which was hanging beside the door: a silvery shimmering lake, with a nymph rising out of it, her hair blonde and wet, to smile at a peasant boy who stood hiding among very green bushes. I could half see the nymph's left breast, and her neck was very white and a little too long.

I don't know when it was, but later I put my hand on the door handle and even before I pressed it down and slowly pushed the door open I knew that Anna was mine: her face was completely covered with small, bluish, shimmering scars, a smell of mushrooms stewing in the pan came out of her room, and I opened the door wide, put my hand on Anna's shoulder, and tried to smile.

STORY IN REVERSE

ILSE AICHINGER

Translated by Christopher Levenson

SPIEGELGESCHICHTE

WENN einer dein Bett aus dem Saal schiebt, wenn du siehst, daß der Himmel grün wird, und wenn du dem Vikar die Leichenrede ersparen willst, so ist es Zeit für dich, aufzustehen, leise, wie Kinder aufstehen, wenn am Morgen Licht durch die Läden schimmert, heimlich, daß es die Schwester nicht sieht – und schnell!

Aber da hat er schon begonnen, der Vikar, da hörst du seine Stimme, jung und eifrig und unaufhaltsam, da hörst du ihn schon reden. Laß es geschehen! Laß seine guten Worte untertauchen in dem blinden Regen. Dein Grab ist offen. Laß seine schnelle Zuversicht erst hilflos werden, daß ihr geholfen wird. Wenn du ihn läßt, wird er am Ende nicht mehr wissen, ob er schon begonnen hat. Und weil er es nicht weiß, gibt er den Trägern das Zeichen. Und die Träger fragen nicht viel und holen deinen Sarg wieder herauf. Und sie nehmen den Kranz vom Deckel und geben ihn dem jungen Mann zurück, der mit gesenktem Kopf am Rand des Grabes steht. Der junge Mann nimmt seinen Kranz und streicht verlegen alle Bänder glatt, er hebt für einen Augenblick die Stirne, und da wirft ihm der Regen ein paar Tränen über die Wangen. Dann bewegt sich der Zug die Mauern entlang wieder zurück. Die Kerzen in der kleinen, häßlichen Kapelle werden noch einmal angezündet und der Vikar sagt die Totengebete, damit du leben kannst. Er schüttelt dem jungen Mann heftig die Hand und wünscht ihm vor Verlegenheit viel Glück. Es ist sein erstes Begräbnis, und er errötet bis zum Hals hinunter. Und ehe er sich verbessern kann, ist auch

STORY IN REVERSE

IF someone pushes your bed out of the ward, if you see that the sky is turning green, and if you want to spare the curate the trouble of a funeral sermon, then it is time you got up, as quietly as children get up when the light shimmers through the shutters in the morning, stealthily, so that the sister does not see you—and quickly!

But too late, the curate has already begun; there you can hear his voice, young and eager and interminable, you can hear him talking already. So be it! Let his good words be submerged in the blinding rain. Your grave is open. Let his brisk confidence first become helpless, so that it can be helped. If you leave him, at the end he won't know any longer if he has already started. And because he does not know he gives a sign to the pall-bearers. And the pall-bearers ask no questions but lift your coffin out again. And they take the wreath from the coffin-lid and return it to the young man who is standing with bowed head at the edge of the grave. The young man takes his wreath and in his embarrassment smooths out all the ribbons; he looks up for a moment and the rain dashes a few tears across his cheeks. Then the procession moves back along the walls. The candles in the ugly little chapel are relit and the curate says the prayer for the dead, in order that you may live. He shakes the young man vigorously by the hand and in his embarrassment wishes him every happiness. It is his first funeral and he is blushing right down to his collar. And before he can correct himself the young man

der junge Mann verschwunden. Was bleibt jetzt zu tun? Wenn einer einem Trauernden viel Glück gewünscht hat, bleibt ihm nichts übrig, als den Toten wieder heimzuschicken.

Gleich darauf fährt der Wagen mit deinem Sarg die lange Straße wieder hinauf. Links und rechts sind Häuser, und an allen Fenstern stehen gelbe Narzissen, wie sie ja auch in alle Kränze gewunden sind, dagegen ist nichts zu machen. Kinder pressen ihre Gesichter an die verschlossenen Scheiben, es regnet, aber eins davon wird trotzdem aus der Haustür laufen. Es hängt sich hinten an den Leichenwagen, wird abgeworfen und bleibt zurück. Das Kind legt beide Hände über die Augen und schaut euch böse nach. Wo soll denn eins sich aufschwingen, solang es auf der Friedhofsstraße wohnt?

Dein Wagen wartet an der Kreuzung auf das grüne Licht. Es regnet schwächer. Die Tropfen tanzen auf dem Wagendach. Das Heu riecht aus der Ferne. Die Straßen sind frisch getauft, und der Himmel legt seine Hand auf alle Dächer. Dein Wagen fährt aus reiner Höflichkeit ein Stück neben der Trambahn her. Zwei kleine Jungen am Straßenrand wetten um ihre Ehre. Aber der auf die Trambahn gesetzt hat, wird verlieren. Du hättest ihn warnen können, aber um dieser Ehre willen ist noch keiner aus dem Sarg gestiegen.

Sei geduldig. Es ist ja Frühsommer. Da reicht der Morgen noch lange in die Nacht hinein. Ihr kommt zurecht. Bevor es dunkel wird und alle Kinder von den Straßenrändern verschwunden sind, biegt auch der Wagen schon in den Spitalshof ein, ein Streifen Mond fällt zugleich in die Einfahrt. Gleich kommen die Männer und heben deinen Sarg vom Leichenwagen. Und der Leichenwagen fährt fröhlich nach Hause.

Sie tragen deinen Sarg durch die zweite Einfahrt über

is gone. What can one do now? If one wishes a mourner every happiness, there is nothing for it but to send the dead person home again.

Straight afterwards the hearse with your coffin drives back up the long street. To the left and right there are houses with yellow narcissi blooming in every window, the sort that is worked into every wreath; there is nothing one can do about it. Children press their faces against the shut panes. It is raining, but in spite of that one of them is going to run out of the front door. He hangs on to the back of the hearse, is thrust off, and stays behind. The child covers its eyes with both hands and angrily watches you go. But where else can one swing if one lives in the street that leads to the cemetery?

Your car is waiting for the green light at the cross-roads. The rain is easing off. The raindrops dance off the car roof. There is a smell of distant hay. The streets are freshly christened, the sky is placing its hand on all the roofs. Out of sheer gallantry your car drives for a while alongside the tram. Two little boys at the kerb are staking their honour on which is the faster. But the one who has bet on the tram is going to lose. You might have warned him, but no one has yet for the sake of this honour arisen from his coffin.

Have patience. After all, it is early summer. The morning still reaches far back into the night. You arrive in time. Before it is dark and all the children have vanished from the kerbs, the car turns into the courtyard of the hospital, a ray of moonlight falls directly on to the entrance. Soon the men come and lift your coffin from the hearse. And the hearse drives cheerfully home.

They carry your coffin through the second entrance across the court and into the mortuary. There the empty catafalque, black and lopsided and raised, is waiting,

den Hof in die Leichenhalle. Dort wartet der leere Sockel schwarz und schief und erhöht, und sie setzen den Sarg darauf und öffnen ihn wieder, und einer von ihnen flucht, weil die Nägel zu fest eingeschlagen sind. Diese verdammte Gründlichkeit!

Gleich darauf kommt auch der junge Mann und bringt den Kranz zurück, es war schon hohe Zeit. Die Männer ordnen die Schleifen und legen ihn vorne hin, da kannst du ruhig sein, der Kranz liegt gut. Bis morgen sind die welken Blüten frisch und schließen sich zu Knospen. Die Nacht über bleibst du allein, das Kreuz zwischen den Händen, und auch den Tag über wirst du viel Ruhe haben. Du wirst es später lange nicht mehr fertig bringen, so still zu liegen.

Am nächsten Tag kommt der junge Mann wieder. Und weil der Regen ihm keine Tränen gibt, starrt er ins Leere und dreht die Mütze zwischen seinen Fingern. Erst bevor sie den Sarg wieder auf das Brett heben, schlägt er die Hände vor das Gesicht. Er weint. Du bleibst nicht länger in der Leichenhalle. Warum weint er? Der Sargdeckel liegt nur mehr lose, und es ist heller Morgen. Die Spatzen schreien fröhlich. Sie wissen nicht, daß es verboten ist, die Toten zu erwecken. Der junge Mann geht vor deinem Sarg her, als stünden Gläser zwischen seinen Schritten. Der Wind ist kühl und verspielt, ein unmündiges Kind.[1]

Sie tragen dich ins Haus und die Stiegen hinauf. Du wirst aus dem Sarg gehoben. Dein Bett ist frisch gerichtet. Der junge Mann starrt durch das Fenster in den Hof hinunter, da paaren sich zwei Tauben und gurren laut, geekelt wendet er sich ab.

Und da haben sie dich schon in das Bett zurückgelegt. Und sie haben dir das Tuch wieder um den Mund gebunden, und das Tuch macht dich so fremd. Der Mann

and they set the coffin on it and open it again, and one of them curses because the nails have been hammered in too firmly. This damned thoroughness!

Soon afterwards the young man also comes and returns the wreath. It was high time. The men arrange the ribbons and place them at the front; there now, you can relax, the wreath is in good order. By morning the faded blooms will be fresh and closed up in buds. During the night you remain alone with the cross between your hands, and by day too you will have plenty of peace. Later on you will not manage to lie nearly so still.

Next day the young man comes again. And because the rain gives him no tears he stares into the emptiness and twists his cap between his fingers. Only when they are about to raise the coffin on to the bier again does he cover his face with his hands. He is crying. You remain no longer in the mortuary. What is he crying for? The coffin lid is now loose and it is broad daylight. The sparrows twitter joyfully. They do not know that it is forbidden to awaken the dead. The young man walks in front of your coffin as though glasses stood between his steps. The wind is cool and playful like a romping child.[1]

They carry you into the house and up the stairs. You are lifted out of the coffin. Your bed has been freshly made. The young man stares through the window into the courtyard where two doves are mating and cooing loudly; he turns away in disgust.

And now they have laid you back in bed. And they have bound a cloth over your mouth, and the cloth makes you look so strange. The man begins to scream and throw himself upon you. They lead him gently away. 'Silence must be observed' is written on all the walls, the hospitals are overcrowded nowadays, the dead must not awake too soon.

beginnt zu schreien und wirft sich über dich. Sie führen ihn sachte weg. «Bewahret Ruhe!»[2] steht an allen Wänden, die Krankenhäuser sind zur Zeit überfüllt, die Toten dürfen nicht zu früh erwachen.

Vom Hafen heulen die Schiffe. Zur Abfahrt oder zur Ankunft? Wer soll das wissen? Still! Bewahret Ruhe! Erweckt die Toten nicht, bevor es Zeit ist, die Toten haben einen leisen Schlaf. Doch die Schiffe heulen weiter. Und ein wenig später werden sie dir das Tuch vom Kopf nehmen müssen, ob sie es wollen oder nicht. Und sie werden dich waschen und deine Hemden wechseln, und einer von ihnen wird sich schnell über dein Herz beugen, schnell, solang du noch tot bist. Es ist nicht mehr viel Zeit, und daran sind die Schiffe schuld. Der Morgen wird schon dunkler. Sie öffnen deine Augen und die funkeln weiß. Sie sagen jetzt auch nichts mehr davon, daß du friedlich aussiehst, dem Himmel sei Dank dafür, es erstirbt ihnen im Mund. Warte noch! Gleich sind sie gegangen. Keiner will Zeuge sein, denn[3] dafür wird man heute noch verbrannt.[4]

Sie lassen dich allein. So allein lassen sie dich, daß du die Augen aufschlägst und den grünen Himmel siehst, so allein lassen sie dich, daß du zu atmen beginnst, schwer und röchelnd und tief, rasselnd wie eine Ankerkette, wenn sie sich löst. Du bäumst dich auf und schreist nach deiner Mutter. Wie grün der Himmel ist!

«Die Fieberträume lassen nach», sagt eine Stimme hinter dir, «der Todeskampf beginnt!»

Ach die! Was wissen die?

Geh jetzt! Jetzt ist der Augenblick! Alle sind weggerufen. Geh, eh sie wiederkommen und eh ihr Flüstern wieder laut wird, geh die Stiegen hinunter, an dem Pförtner vorbei, durch den Morgen, der Nacht wird. Die Vögel schreien in der Finsternis, als hätten deine Schmerzen

The ships hoot in the harbour. Arriving or departing? Who knows? Hush! Silence must be observed. Don't awake the dead before their time, the dead sleep lightly. But the ships continue to hoot. And a little later they will have to take that cloth from your head, whether they like it or not. And they will wash you and change your shirts, and one of them will bend quickly over your heart, quickly, while you are still dead. There is not much more time, and that is the fault of the ships. The morning is already getting darker. They open your eyes, which flash whitely. They don't say anything more about your looking peaceful, thank heavens for that, the words stick in their throats. Wait a little. Soon they will be gone. No one wants to be a witness, because people are burnt for this even today.

They leave you alone. They leave you so much alone that you open your eyes and see the green sky, they leave you so much alone that you begin to breathe, heavy and gasping and deep, rattling like an anchor chain when it is cast. You rear up and shout for your mother. How green the sky is!

'The delirium is subsiding,' says a voice behind you, 'the death throes are beginning.'

Oh, them! What do they know about it?

Go now! Now is the moment. They have all been called away. Go before they return, and before their whispers again become loud, go down the steps, past the hall porter, through the morning that is becoming night. The birds scream in the darkness as if your pains had begun to rejoice. Go home! And lie down in your own bed, even though its joints creak and it is still rumpled. There you'll get well more quickly. You rage there against yourself for only three days, and drink your fill of the green sky, for only three days there you

zu jubeln begonnen.[5] Geh nach Hause! Und leg dich in
dein eigenes Bett zurück, auch wenn es in den Fugen
kracht und noch zerwühlt ist. Da wirst du schneller gesund!
Da tobst du nur drei Tage lang gegen dich und trinkst
dich satt am grünen Himmel, da stößt du nur drei Tage
lang die Suppe weg, die dir die Frau von oben bringt, am
vierten nimmst du sie.

Und am siebenten, der der Tag der Ruhe ist, am
siebenten gehst du weg. Die Schmerzen jagen dich, den
Weg wirst du ja finden. Erst links, dann rechts und wieder
links, quer durch die Hafengassen, die so elend sind, daß
sie nicht anders können, als zum Meer zu führen. Wenn
nur der junge Mann in deiner Nähe wäre, aber der junge
Mann ist nicht bei dir, im Sarg warst du viel schöner.
Doch jetzt ist dein Gesicht verzerrt von Schmerzen, die
Schmerzen haben zu jubeln aufgehört.[6] Und jetzt steht
auch der Schweiß wieder auf deiner Stirne, den ganzen
Weg lang, nein, im Sarg, da warst du schöner!

Die Kinder spielen mit den Kugeln am Weg. Du läufst
in sie hinein, du läufst, als liefst du mit dem Rücken nach
vorn, und keines ist dein Kind. Wie soll denn auch eines
davon dein Kind sein, wenn du zur Alten gehst, die bei
der Kneipe wohnt? Das weiß der ganze Hafen, wovon die
Alte ihren Schnaps bezahlt.

Sie steht schon an der Tür. Die Tür ist offen, und sie
streckt dir ihre Hand entgegen, die ist schmutzig. Alles ist
dort schmutzig. Am Kamin stehen die gelben Blumen,
und das sind dieselben, die sie in die Kränze winden, das
sind schon wieder dieselben. Und die Alte ist viel zu
freundlich. Und die Treppen knarren auch hier. Und die
Schiffe heulen, wohin du immer gehst, die heulen überall.
Und die Schmerzen schütteln dich, aber du darfst nicht
schreien. Die Schiffe dürfen heulen, aber du darfst nicht
schreien. Gib der Alten das Geld für den Schnaps! Wenn

push the soup aside that the woman upstairs brings you, and on the fourth day you take it.

And on the seventh day, which is the day of rest, you go away. The pain drives you on, you will find the way. First left, then right, then left again, right through the dockside alleys, which are so poverty-stricken that they can do nothing else but lead to the sea. If only the young man were near you, but the young man is not with you, in the coffin you were much more beautiful. But now your face is distorted by pain, the pain has stopped rejoicing. And now too – the whole way – the sweat stands out on your forehead; no, you were much more beautiful in the coffin.

The children are playing marbles in the street. You run into them, you run as if you were running back to front and none of them is your child. How could one of them be yours, when you are going to the old woman who lives next to the pub? The whole harbour knows how the old woman pays for her *Schnaps*.

She is already standing at the door. The door is open and she reaches out her hand to you. Her hand is dirty. Everything there is dirty. On the hearth stand the yellow flowers, and they are the same ones that they work into wreathes, they are the same ones again. And the old woman is much too friendly. And the stairs creak here as well. And wherever you go the ships wail, they wail everywhere. And the pain shakes you but you must not cry out. Give the old woman the money for the *Schnaps*! When once you have given her the money, she holds your mouth shut with both her hands. She is quite sober from all her *Schnaps*, the old woman. She doesn't dream of the unborn. The innocent children dare not complain of it to the saints and the guilty ones dare not do so either. But you – you dare!

du ihr erst das Geld gegeben hast, hält sie dir deinen Mund mit beiden Händen zu. Die ist ganz nüchtern von dem vielen Schnaps, die Alte. Die träumt nicht von den Ungeborenen. Die unschuldigen Kinder wagen's nicht, sie bei den Heiligen zu verklagen, und die schuldigen wagen's auch nicht. Aber du – du wagst es!

«Mach mir mein Kind wieder lebendig!»

Das hat noch keine von der Alten verlangt. Aber du verlangst es. Der Spiegel gibt dir Kraft. Der blinde Spiegel mit den Fliegenflecken läßt dich verlangen, was noch keine verlangt hat.

«Mach es lebendig, sonst stoß ich deine gelben Blumen um, sonst kratz ich dir die Augen aus, sonst reiß ich deine Fenster auf und schrei über die Gasse, damit sie hören müssen, was sie wissen, ich schrei – »

Und da erschrickt die Alte. Und in dem großen Schrecken, in dem blinden Spiegel erfüllt sie deine Bitte. Sie weiß nicht, was sie tut, doch in dem blinden Spiegel gelingt es ihr. Die Angst wird furchtbar, und die Schmerzen beginnen endlich wieder zu jubeln. Und eh du schreist, weißt du das Wiegenlied: Schlaf, Kindlein, schlaf! Und eh du schreist, stürzt dich der Spiegel die finsteren Treppen wieder hinab und läßt dich gehen, laufen läßt er dich. Lauf nicht zu schnell!

Heb lieber deinen Blick vom Boden auf, sonst könnt es sein, daß du da drunten an den Planken um den leeren Bauplatz in einen Mann hineinläufst, in einen jungen Mann, der seine Mütze dreht. Daran erkennst du ihn. Das ist derselbe, der zuletzt an deinem Sarg die Mütze gedreht hat, da ist er schon wieder! Da steht er, als wäre er nie weggewesen, da lehnt er an den Planken. Du fällst in seine Arme. Er hat schon wieder keine Tränen, gib ihm von den deinen. Und nimm Abschied, eh du dich an seinen Arm hängst. Nimm von ihm Abschied! Du wirst es nicht

38

'Bring my child back to life again!'

Nobody has ever asked that of the old woman before. But you ask it. The mirror gives you power. The blind mirror with the fly dirt permits you to ask what no one has asked before.

'Bring it back to life, otherwise I'll knock over your yellow flowers, otherwise I'll scratch your eyes out, otherwise I'll wrench your window open and shout across the alleyway, so that they all have to hear what they know already, I'll scream –'

At that, the old woman becomes alarmed. And in her great alarm, in the blind mirror, she grants your request. She does not know what she is doing but in the blind mirror she succeeds. The fear becomes terrible and the pain is beginning to rejoice again at last. And before you can scream you know the lullaby, 'Sleep, little child, sleep!', and before you can scream the mirror hurls you down the dark stairs again and makes you walk away, makes you run. Don't run too fast!

You had better raise your eyes from the ground, otherwise it might happen that, down there by the fence around the empty building site, you run into a man, a young man, who is twisting his cap between his hands. That is how you recognize him. He is the same one who was recently twisting his cap in his hands beside your coffin; there he is again! There he stands as if he had never gone away, there he is, leaning against the fence. You fall into his arms. Once again he has no tears; give him some of yours. And bid him farewell before you take his arm. Take leave of him. You won't forget it even if he forgets: at the beginning one takes one's leave. Before you go any farther with one another, you must part for ever at the fence that surrounds the empty building site.

vergessen, wenn er es auch vergißt: Am Anfang nimmt man Abschied. Ehe man miteinander weitergeht, muß man sich an den Planken um den leeren Bauplatz für immer trennen.

Dann geht ihr weiter. Es gibt da einen Weg, der an den Kohlenlagern vorbei zur See führt. Ihr schweigt. Du wartest auf das erste Wort, du läßt es ihm, damit dir nicht das letzte bleibt. Was wird er sagen? Schnell, eh ihr an der See seid, die unvorsichtig macht! Was sagt er? Was ist das erste Wort? Kann es denn so schwer sein, daß es ihn stammeln läßt, daß es ihn zwingt, den Blick zu senken? Oder sind es die Kohlenberge, die über die Planken ragen und ihm Schatten unter die Augen werfen und ihn mit ihrer Schwärze blenden? Das erste Wort – jetzt hat er es gesagt: es ist der Name einer Gasse. So heißt die Gasse, in der die Alte wohnt. Kann denn das sein? Bevor er weiß, daß du das Kind erwartest, nennt er dir schon die Alte, bevor er sagt, daß er dich liebt, nennt er die Alte. Sei ruhig! Er weiß nicht, daß du bei der Alten schon gewesen bist, er kann es auch nicht wissen, er weiß nichts von dem Spiegel. Aber kaum hat er's gesagt, hat er es auch vergessen. Im Spiegel sagt man alles, daß es vergessen sei. Und kaum hast du gesagt, daß du das Kind erwartest, hast du es auch verschwiegen. Der Spiegel spiegelt alles. Die Kohlenberge[7] weichen hinter euch zurück, da seid ihr an der See und seht die weißen Boote wie Fragen an der Grenze eures Blicks, seid still, die See nimmt euch die Antwort aus dem Mund, die See verschlingt, was ihr noch sagen wolltet.

Von da ab geht ihr viele Male den Strand hinauf, als ob ihr ihn hinabgingt, nach Hause, als ob ihr wegließt, und weg, als gingt ihr heim.

Was flüstern die in ihren hellen Hauben? «Das ist der Todeskampf!» Die laßt nur reden.

Eines Tages wird der Himmel blaß genug sein, so blaß,

Then you walk on. There is a path there which leads past the coal-yards to the sea. You are both silent. You are waiting for the first word, you let him have it so that you are not left with the last one. What will he say? Quickly, before you are by the sea that makes you careless. What is he saying? What is that first word? Can it be so difficult then, that it makes him stammer, that it forces him to lower his gaze? Or is it the coal-tips that loom up over the fence and cast shadows across his eyes and dazzle him with their blackness? The first word – now he has said it: it is the name of a street. That is the name of the alley in which the old woman lives. How is that? Before he knows that you are expecting a child, he has mentioned the old woman, before he says that he loves you, he mentions the old woman's name. Keep calm! He does not know that you have already been to the old woman, he can't know it either, he knows nothing about the mirror. And he has scarcely said it before he has forgotten it. In the mirror everything is said in order that it may be forgotten. And you have scarcely said that you are expecting a child before you have suppressed the news. The mirror reflects everything. The coal-tips fade away behind you, there you both are by the sea and you see the white boats like questions on the edge of your gaze. Be still, the sea takes the answer out of your mouth, the sea swallows up whatever else it was you still wanted to say.

From there you go up the beach many times as if you were going down it, homewards as if you were running away from it, and away from it as if you were walking home.

What are they whispering in their bright hoods? 'Those are the death throes.' Just let them talk!

One day the sky will be pale enough, so pale that its

daß seine Blässe glänzen wird. Gibt es denn einen anderen Glanz als den der letzten Blässe?

An diesem Tag spiegelt der blinde Spiegel das verdammte Haus. Verdammt nennen die Leute ein Haus, das abgerissen wird, verdammt nennen sie das, sie wissen es nicht besser. Es soll euch nicht erschrecken. Der Himmel ist jetzt blaß genug. Und wie der Himmel in der Blässe erwartet auch das Haus am Ende der Verdammung die Seligkeit. Vom vielen Lachen kommen leicht die Tränen. Du hast genug geweint. Nimm deinen Kranz zurück. Jetzt wirst du auch die Zöpfe bald wieder lösen dürfen. Alles ist im Spiegel. Und hinter allem, was ihr tut, liegt grün die See. Wenn ihr das Haus verlaßt, liegt sie vor euch. Wenn ihr durch die eingesunkenen Fenster wieder aussteigt, habt ihr vergessen. Im Spiegel tut man alles, daß es vergeben sei.

Von da ab drängt er dich, mit ihm hineinzugehen. Aber in dem Eifer entfernt ihr euch davon und biegt vom Strand ab. Ihr wendet euch nicht um. Und das verdammte Haus bleibt hinter euch zurück. Ihr geht den Fluß hinauf, und euer eigenes Fieber fließt euch entgegen, es fließt an euch vorbei. Gleich läßt sein Drängen nach. Und in demselben Augenblick bist du nicht mehr bereit, ihr werdet scheuer. Das ist die Ebbe, die die See von allen Küsten wegzieht. Sogar die Flüsse sinken zur Zeit der Ebbe. Und drüben auf der anderen Seite lösen die Wipfel endlich die Krone ab. Weiße Schindeldächer schlafen darunter.

Gib acht, jetzt beginnt er bald von der Zukunft zu reden, von den vielen Kindern und vom langen Leben, und seine Wangen brennen vor Eifer. Sie zünden auch die deinen an. Ihr werdet streiten, ob ihr Söhne oder Töchter wollt, und du willst lieber Söhne. Und er wollte sein Dach lieber mit Ziegeln decken, und du willst lieber – aber da seid ihr den Fluß schon viel zu weit hinauf gegangen. Der

paleness will shine. Is there then any other splendour than that of the ultimate paleness?

On this day the blind mirror reflects the condemned house. 'Condemned' is what people call a house that is to be demolished, they call it condemned, they know no better. It should not frighten you. The sky is pale enough now. And like the sky in its paleness the house too awaits the bliss at the end of its condemnation. After much laughter tears come easily. You have cried enough. Take your wreath back. Soon you will be allowed to loose your pigtails. Everything is in the mirror. And behind everything that you do the sea lies green. When you leave the house together it spreads out before you. When you climb out again through the caving-in windows you have forgotten. In the mirror everything is done that it may be forgiven.

From then onwards he urges you to go inside with him. But in your eagerness you leave the house behind and turn away from the beach. You do not turn round. And the condemned house remains behind you. You walk towards the river and your own fever flows towards you, flows past you. Soon his entreaties subside, and at that very moment you are no longer ready, you both become shyer. That is the ebb that draws the sea away from all coasts. Even the rivers sink at the time of the ebb, and over there on the other side the tips of trees at last take the place of their crowns. White shingled roofs sleep under them.

Take care, now he will start talking about the future, about lots of children, and a long life, and his cheeks will flush with enthusiasm. They set yours alight too. You will argue about whether you want sons or daughters, and you would prefer sons. And he wants his roof tiled whereas you would prefer . . . but now you have gone

Schrecken packt euch. Die Schindeldächer auf der anderen Seite sind verschwunden, da drüben sind nur mehr Auen und feuchte Wiesen. Und hier? Gebt auf den Weg acht. Es dämmert – so nüchtern, wie es nur am Morgen dämmert. Die Zukunft ist vorbei. Die Zukunft ist ein Weg am Fluß, der in die Auen mündet. Geht zurück!

Was soll jetzt werden?

Drei Tage später wagt er nicht mehr, den Arm um deine Schultern zu legen. Wieder drei Tage später fragt er dich, wie du heißt, und du fragst ihn. Nun wißt ihr voneinander nicht einmal mehr die Namen. Und ihr fragt auch nicht mehr. Es ist schöner so. Seid ihr nicht zum Geheimnis geworden?

Jetzt geht ihr endlich wieder schweigsam nebeneinander her. Wenn er dich jetzt noch etwas fragt, so fragt er, ob es regnen wird. Wer kann das wissen? Ihr werdet immer fremder. Von der Zukunft habt ihr schon lange zu reden aufgehört. Ihr seht euch nur mehr selten, aber noch immer seid ihr einander nicht fremd genug. Wartet, seid geduldig. Eines Tages wird es so weit sein. Eines Tages ist er dir so fremd, daß du ihn auf einer finsteren Gasse vor einem offenen Tor zu lieben beginnst. Alles will seine Zeit.[8] Jetzt ist sie da.

«Es dauert nicht mehr lang», sagen die hinter dir, «es geht zu Ende!»

Was wissen die? Beginnt nicht jetzt erst alles?

Ein Tag wird kommen, da siehst du ihn zum erstenmal. Und er sieht dich. Zum erstenmal, das heißt: Nie wieder. Aber erschreckt nicht! Ihr müßt nicht voneinander Abschied nehmen, das habt ihr längst getan. Wie gut es ist, daß ihr es schon getan habt!

Es wird ein Herbsttag sein, voller Erwartung darauf, daß alle Früchte wieder Blüten werden, wie er schon ist, der Herbst, mit diesem hellen Rauch und mit den Schatten,

too far up the river. You are gripped by fear. The shingled roofs on the other side have disappeared. Now there are only pastures and damp meadows over there. And here? Keep your eyes on the path. It is becoming dusk, as dully as only day can dawn. The future is past. The future is a path by the riverside which peters out in the meadows. Go back!

What is to happen now?

Three days later he no longer dares to place his arm around your shoulder. Another three days and he asks you your name and you his. Now you do not even know each other's name. And you don't even ask any longer. It is better so. Have you not become mysteries to each other?

Now at last again you walk in silence side by side. If he should ask you anything now he will ask you if it is going to rain. Who can tell? You become ever more estranged. You have long since given up talking about the future. You see each other now only seldom, but you are still not estranged enough from each other. Wait, be patient. One day that stage will be reached. One day he will be so much of a stranger to you that you begin to love him in a dark alleyway before an open gateway. Everything has its due time and place. Now it has come.

'It won't last much longer,' they say behind you, 'the end is approaching.'

What do they know about it? Isn't everything only just beginning?

A day will come when you see him for the first time. And he sees you. For the first time, that is to say, never again. But do not be afraid. You need not take leave of one another, you did that long ago. How good it is that you have already done so!

It will be an autumn day, full of expectation that all

die wie Splitter zwischen den Schritten liegen, daß du die
Füße daran zerschneiden könntest, daß du darüberfällst,
wenn du um Äpfel auf den Markt geschickt bist, du fällst
vor Hoffnung und vor Fröhlichkeit. Ein junger Mann
kommt dir zu Hilfe. Er hat die Jacke nur lose umgeworfen
und lächelt und dreht die Mütze und weiß kein Wort zu
sagen. Aber ihr seid sehr fröhlich in diesem letzten Licht.
Du dankst ihm und wirfst ein wenig den Kopf zurück,
und da lösen sich die aufgesteckten Zöpfe und fallen
herab. «Ach,» sagt er, «gehst du nicht noch zur Schule?»
Er dreht sich um und geht und pfeift ein Lied. So trennt
ihr euch, ohne einander nur noch einmal anzuschauen,
ganz ohne Schmerz und ohne es zu wissen, daß ihr euch
trennt.

Jetzt darfst du wieder mit deinen kleinen Brüdern
spielen, und du darfst mit ihnen den Fluß entlanggehen,
den Weg am Fluß unter den Erlen, und drüben sind die
weißen Schindeldächer wie immer zwischen den Wipfeln.
Was bringt die Zukunft? Keine Söhne. Brüder hat sie dir
gebracht, Zöpfe, um sie tanzen zu lassen, Bälle, um zu
fliegen. Sei ihr nicht böse, es ist das Beste, was sie hat.
Die Schule kann beginnen.

Noch bist du zu wenig groß, noch mußt du auf dem
Schulhof während der großen Pause in Reihen gehen und
flüstern und erröten und durch die Finger lachen. Aber
warte noch ein Jahr, und du darfst wieder über die Schnüre
springen und nach den Zweigen haschen, die über die
Mauern hängen.[9] Die fremden Sprachen hast du schon
gelernt, doch so leicht bleibt es nicht. Deine eigene
Sprache ist viel schwerer. Noch schwerer wird es sein,
lesen und schreiben zu lernen, doch am schwersten ist es,
alles zu vergessen. Und wenn du bei der ersten Prüfung
alles wissen mußtest, so darfst du doch am Ende nichts
mehr wissen. Wirst du das bestehen? Wirst du still genug

the fruits will again become blossoms, as it always is, the autumn with this bright smoke and with the shadows that lie like splinters between one's steps, so that you could cut your feet on them, so that you could fall over them when you are sent to the market for apples, you could fall down for sheer hope and happiness. A young man comes to help you. He has slung his jacket loosely about him and smiles and twists his cap in his hands and does not know what to say. But you are very happy in this last light. You thank him and throw your head back a little, and the pinned-up plaits come undone and fall down. 'Ah,' he says, 'aren't you still at school?' He turns round and goes off, whistling a tune. So you part, without looking at each other even once again, quite without pain and without knowing that you are parting.

Now you may play with your little brothers again and you may walk with them beside the river, the path by the river under the alders, and over there, as always, are the white shingle roofs between the tree-tops. What does the future bring? No sons. It has brought you brothers, pigtails to swing, balls to hurl. Don't be angry with the future, that is the best it has. School can start.

You are still not big enough, you must still walk around the playground in crocodiles during the long break and whisper and blush and laugh between your fingers. But wait another year and you'll be allowed to jump over the skipping-rope and snatch at the twigs that hang over the walls. You have already learnt foreign languages but it's not as easy as it was. Your own language is much more difficult. It will be much more difficult learning to read and write, but the most difficult of all is forgetting everything. And if you had to know everything at the first exam, now at the end

sein? Wenn du genug Furcht hast, um den Mund nicht aufzutun, wird alles gut.

Du hängst den blauen Hut, den alle Schulkinder tragen, wieder an den Nagel und verläßt die Schule. Es ist wieder Herbst. Die Blüten sind lange schon zu Knospen geworden, die Knospen zu nichts und nichts wieder zu Früchten. Überall gehen kleine Kinder nach Hause, die ihre Prüfung bestanden haben, wie du. Ihr alle wißt nichts mehr. Du gehst nach Hause, dein Vater erwartet dich, und die kleinen Brüder schreien so laut sie können und zerren an deinem Haar. Du bringst sie zur Ruhe[10] und tröstest deinen Vater.

Bald kommt der Sommer mit den langen Tagen. Bald stirbt deine Mutter. Du und dein Vater, ihr beide holt sie vom Friedhof ab. Drei Tage liegt sie noch zwischen den knisternden Kerzen, wie damals du. Blast alle Kerzen aus, eh sie erwacht! Aber sie riecht das Wachs und hebt sich auf die Arme und klagt leise über die Verschwendung. Dann steht sie auf und wechselt ihre Kleider.

Es ist gut, daß deine Mutter gestorben ist, denn länger hättest du es mit den kleinen Brüdern allein nicht machen können. Doch jetzt ist sie da. Jetzt besorgt sie alles und lehrt dich auch das Spielen noch viel besser, man kann es nie gut genug können. Es ist keine leichte Kunst. Aber das schwerste ist es noch immer nicht.

Das schwerste bleibt es doch, das Sprechen zu vergessen und das Gehen zu verlernen, hilflos zu stammeln und auf dem Boden zu kriechen, um zuletzt in Windeln gewickelt zu werden. Das schwerste bleibt es, alle Zärtlichkeiten zu ertragen und nur mehr zu schauen. Sei geduldig! Bald ist alles gut. Gott weiß den Tag, an dem du schwach genug bist.

Es ist der Tag deiner Geburt. Du kommst zur Welt und schlägst die Augen auf und schließt sie wieder vor dem

you are allowed to know nothing more. Will you pass? Will you be calm enough? If you are afraid enough not to open your mouth all will go well.

You hang the blue hat that all schoolchildren wear on the peg again and leave the school. It is autumn again. The blossoms have already long since become buds, the buds have become nothing, and the nothing fruit again. Everywhere little children who, like you, have passed their exams, are going home. You all know nothing any more. You go home, your father is waiting for you and your little brothers shout at the tops of their voices and pull your hair. You calm them down and comfort your father.

Soon the summer comes with its long days. Soon your mother dies. You and your father, the two of you, take her away from the cemetery. Three days long she lies between the spluttering candles as you did then. Blow all the candles out before she wakes. But she smells the wax and raises herself on her arms and complains quietly about the wastage. Then she gets up and changes her clothes.

It is a good thing your mother has died, for you could not have managed much longer alone with your little brothers. But now she is there. Now she takes charge of everything and teaches you to play much better, one can never be too good at it. It is not an easy art, but it is by no means the most difficult.

The hardest thing, however, remains: to forget how to speak and to lose the knack of walking, to splutter helplessly and crawl on the floor, and finally to be wrapped in nappies. The hardest thing is to bear all the tenderness and only look on. Be patient, soon everything will be all right. God knows the day when you will be weak enough.

starken Licht. Das Licht wärmt dir die Glieder, du regst
dich in der Sonne, du bist da, du lebst. Dein Vater beugt
sich über dich.

«Es ist zu Ende –» sagen die hinter dir, «sie ist tot!»

Still! Laß sie reden!

It is the day of your birth. You come into the world and open your eyes and shut them again because of the strong light. The light warms your limbs, you stretch yourself in the sun, you are there, you live. Your father is bending over you.

'The end has come,' they say behind you, 'she is dead.'

Quiet! Let them talk!

THE HOST

HANS BENDER

Translated by Roland Hill

DIE HOSTIE

WARUM hat sie kein anderer gefunden? Warum gerade ich, der ihren Wert weiß, der sich von diesen Dingen so weit entfernt hat?

Ich konnte nicht ahnen, was die Kapsel enthielt. Ich taxierte[1] ein Geldstück, eine Dose, die einem der Dämchen,[2] die die Straße bevölkern, aus der Handtasche gefallen war. Ich dachte an ihren Preis, blieb stehen, sah mich um, ob man mich beobachtete, bückte mich rasch, hob sie auf und steckte sie in die Tasche.

Ich fand sie etwa hundert Meter vor dem Blumengeschäft. Das Schaufenster war erleuchtet. Orchideen standen hinter der Scheibe, Kamelien und fremde Gewächse, deren Namen ich nicht weiß. Vor dem hellen Fenster nahm ich sie aus der Tasche, gelangweilt, selbstverständlich, wie man Zigaretten aus der Tasche holt. Es war eine goldene Kapsel. Ein Kreuz war eingraviert, ein schlankes, hohes Kreuz, dessen Längsbalken einen gravierten Fisch durchschnitt. Ich öffnete die Dose und sah die Hostie. Wer einmal glaubte, daß Christus darin – ich erschrak, schloß die Kapsel, behielt sie in der Hand, weil ich nicht wagte, sie in die Tasche zurückzustecken. Sie sollte nicht zwischen dem Feuerzeug, dem Schlüssel und dem schmutzigen Taschentuch liegen. Die Pfarrer, wußte ich, trugen sie auf der Brust, in einem seidenen Futteral, an einer violetten Kordel. Ich hatte eine Tasche, auf der linken Seite meiner dünnen Jacke – über dem Herzen, dachte ich – dorthin wollte ich sie nehmen.

Aus den Blumen und Gewächsen hinter der Scheibe

THE HOST

WHY couldn't someone else have found it? Why did it have to be me, who knows its significance, who has escaped a long way from things like that?

How was I to know what the little box contained? I guessed that inside there would be a coin, that it was a box which one of the tarts who walk that street had perhaps lost from her handbag. I thought of its value, stopped, looked around to see if anyone was watching, bent down quickly, picked it up, and put it into my pocket.

I found it some hundred yards from the flower-shop. The window was brightly lit. There were orchids behind the pane, camellias and strange plants the names of which I don't know. In front of the bright window I took it out, nonchalantly, casually, as one might pull out a packet of cigarettes. It was a gold box. A cross was engraved on it, slim, tall, with its horizontal arms cutting across an engraved fish. I opened the box and saw the sacred host. If one has once believed that Christ was in that . . . I felt afraid, closed the box and kept it in my hand because I did not dare to put it back into my pocket. It seemed wrong company for lighter, keys, and dirty handkerchief. I knew that priests carried these boxes on their breast, in a silken case, hanging from a purple cord. I had an outside pocket on the left of my thin jacket – near the heart, I thought; that was where I wanted to put it.

From among the flowers and plants behind the pane

tauchte das Gesicht eines Herrn. Es trug eine Brille, in
deren Gläsern sich das Licht brach zu scharfen, halben
Monden. Sein Arm griff durch die Blätter, die Hand hielt
eine Schere, schnitt eine Kamelie vom Stock. Ihre Blüte
fiel nach vorn, fiel zur Scheibe, zu mir. Seine Hand griff
danach. Ich lief davon.

Eigentlich wollte ich nach rechts weitergehen, wo die
Straße zum Bahnhof führt. Ich ging, ohne nachzudenken,
nach links, weil ich immer links ging, weil ich in dieser
Straße so etwas wie zu Hause war. Eine Straße, traurig
wie die Welt. Auf der rechten Seite standen vier oder fünf
Häuser mit Ladengeschäften, einer Obstweingaststätte[3] und
einer Bar im zweiten Stock. Dann folgten Trümmer, bis
zum Ende der Straße. Die Trümmer wurden nur belebt
von einem Kiosk,[4] der in die Steinhaufen geschoben war.
Elisa, die Besitzerin, blieb die Nacht über drinnen, und
wenn man dreimal klopfte, öffnete sie.

Nun durfte ich nicht hineingehen. Ich hatte die Hostie. Ich
mußte eine Kirche suchen, mit einem Pfarrhaus daneben,
und die Kapsel mit der Hostie einem Priester zurückgeben.

Aber, wo war eine Kirche? Ich wußte keine. Vier Jahre
wohnte ich in der Stadt, aber ich wußte keine Kirche. Als
ich aus der Gefangenschaft kam, fand ich keine Angehöri-
gen mehr. Es war gleichgültig, wo ich blieb. Eine Stadt war
besser als ein Dorf. Eine Million Einwohner ergeben eine
Million Möglichkeiten, kalkulierte ich. Und wenn man vor
nichts zurückschreckte und jung war, gab es wirklich viele
Möglichkeiten, an Geld zu kommen. Es war nur schwer, in
der Stadt ein Zimmer zu finden. Drei Monate suchte ich.
Eine Schlafstelle war mir angeboten worden, in einem
Wohnzimmer, wo noch einer schlief. Da wollte ich vor-
übergehend wohnen. Nun wohne ich noch heute da. Vielleicht ist diese Schlafstelle schuld, daß ich vier Jahre in einer

the face of a man appeared. He wore spectacles, the lenses of which refracted the light into sharp half moons. His arm reached through the foliage, the hand held a pair of scissors, cut a camellia from its stem. The flower fell forward towards the pane where I stood. His hand groped for it. I ran away.

Actually I wanted to walk to the right where the street leads to the station. But I went to the left, without further thought, simply because I always turned left here, because I felt kind of at home in this street. It was a depressing street, as depressing as the world. On the right side there were four or five houses with shops, a cider tavern, with a bar on the second floor. After that bomb ruins up to the end of the street. The monotony was interrupted only by a kiosk that had been pushed up against the rubble. Elisa, the owner, used to stay there at night and if you knocked three times she would open up.

I could hardly go there now. I had the sacred host. I had to look for a church with a presbytery, and return the box with the host to a priest.

But where was a church? I didn't know a single one. I had lived in this town for four years, but I did not know a single church. I had been a prisoner of war, and when I came back none of my relatives were to be found. So it didn't matter where I stayed. A town was better than a village. A million inhabitants are like a million possibilities, I thought. And for a young man who was not too particular, there were really quite a few possibilities of coming into money. The only difficulty was to find a room in that town. I looked around for three months. A night's lodging had been offered to me, in a living-room, where another man also slept. I thought of staying there for the time being.

Stadt wohne und nicht weiß, wo eine Kirche ist, daß ich
Nacht für Nacht durch die Lokale streune.[5] Schlafen kann
man dort, aber nicht in Ruhe sitzen, kein Buch lesen oder
eine Sprache lernen. Wasinski, der andere, der da schlief,
auf dem Sofa, während ich einen Federrost mit drei dünn-
gewälzten Matratzen zum Bett hatte, war in der Nacht
nie da. Er kam am Morgen, rauchte eine Zigarette, drehte
sich zur Wand und schnarchte. Als ich keine Unterstützung
mehr bekam, half er mir. Er gab mir Zigaretten, Geld, und
eines Abends nahm er mich mit. Seitdem gingen wir zur
gleichen Stunde schlafen.

Ich dachte gerade an ihn, nun stand er da, stand vor
Elisas Kiosk und grinste.

«Ich hab gewartet,» sagte er.

«Warum?»

«Das wirst du schon sehen. Aber vorerst hab ich Hunger.
Gehst du mit rein?»

«Warum nicht,» sagte ich.

Ich durfte mir nichts anmerken lassen. Wasinski klopfte
dreimal an den Bretterladen, gleich darauf hörten wir
Elisas Stimme, die resolut sagte: «Es ist bereits geschlos-
sen!»

«Mach keinen Quatsch,» sagte Wasinski.

«Ach du!» rief Elisa. Sie drehte den Schlüssel, öffnete
die Tür und lachte.

In der dunklen Ecke standen die beiden Rumänen oder
Ungarn Man wußte es nicht genau. Sie kannten Wasinski
und mich, aber sie beachteten uns heute nicht, sondern
redeten aufeinander ein in ihrem gräßlichen Kauderwelsch.
Elisa schrie dazwischen und kniff Janos, den jüngeren der
beiden, in die Hüfte.

«Die Polizei kommt, wenn ihr so blöde schreit!»

«Zwomal,» sagte Wasinski. Und zu mir: «Du doch
auch?»

Today I am still staying there. Perhaps it was because of these lodgings that I have spent four years in a town and don't know where a church is, that I just loaf about the pubs and cafés night after night. You can sleep there, but you can't sit there in peace, read a book or learn a foreign language. Wasinski, my room mate, slept on the sofa – my bed consisted of a spring frame and three worn mattresses; he was always out at night. He came back in the morning, smoked a cigarette, turned to the wall and snored. When I stopped getting assistance, he helped me out, with cigarettes and money. One evening he took me along with him. Since then we have turned in at the same time.

I was just thinking of him and there he was outside Elisa's kiosk, grinning.

'I've been waiting,' he said.

'Why?'

'That you'll know in time. First I want to eat. Coming in?'

'Why not,' I said.

I must not betray myself. Wasinski knocked on the wooden shutters three times, then we heard Elisa's voice saying firmly: 'We're already closed.'

'Don't be daft,' said Wasinski.

'Oh, it's you!' called Elisa. She turned the key, opened the door and laughed.

In the dark corner were the two Rumanians or Hungarians. One couldn't tell where they came from. They knew Wasinski and me, but today they took no notice of us; they went on chattering in their awful lingo. Elisa added her shouts, and dug Janos, the younger one, in the side.

'The cops will be coming if you make such a bloody row.'

Ich sagte: «Eigentlich hab ich keinen Hunger. Ich hab auch nicht soviel Geld bei mir.»

«Nicht soviel Geld! Nicht soviel Geld! Du spinnst wohl! Du hast doch gestern den ganzen Rahm abgeschöpft!»[6]

Ja, ich hatte kein Geld mehr. Ich hatte den Gewinn der vergangenen Nacht Frau Röser gegeben und die Wäsche bezahlt, weil ich nicht gern Schulden hatte, weil ich ihr vorwurfsvolles Gesicht nicht mehr sehen konnte, weil ich endlich wieder einmal ein frisches Hemd auf dem Leib haben wollte. Ich hatte vier Zehnpfennigstücke in der Tasche und hatte – die Kapsel. Wenn ich wollte, konnte ich sie verkaufen. Die beiden Gauner neben mir handelten mit so was. Aus ihren Taschen quollen die Uhren, die Ringe, die Schmucksachen. Ihre Brieftaschen platzten vor Geldscheinen. Wenn etwas blinkte, fielen sie darüber her wie die Elstern.

Elisa schob die Würstchen auf die Theke. Sie lagen heiß auf Kartontellerchen mit einer Scheibe Brot und einem Klacks Senf.

«Hier, ihr Brüder,» sagte sie.

Wasinski steckte gleich beide Würstchen ins Maul. Er widerte mich an.

«Na, keinen Appetit?» fragte er.

«Doch.»

«Wenn es wegen des Geldes ist, kannst du gleich mitkommen!» sagte er.

«Nein, es geht nicht.»

«Warum nicht?»

«Nein, nein, bestimmt nicht! Nicht jetzt. Nicht gleich!»

«Gut,» sagte Wasinski, «dann kommst du eben später. Sagen wir um elf. Hörst du, um elf bei den Taxis.»

«Ja, um elf bei den Taxis.»

Ich biß in meine zweite Wurst. Wasinski musterte mich von oben bis unten.

'Twice,' ordered Wasinski. And to me: 'You'll have some, too?'

I said: 'I'm not really hungry. Anyway, I haven't got enough money on me.'

'Not enough money! Not enough money! You must be cracked. You had the whole rake-off yesterday!'

I really did have no money left. I had given the proceeds of the previous night to Frau Röser and paid for the washing, because I'd had just about enough of seeing her reproachful face, and because I felt it was time to put on a clean shirt again. I had four ten-pfennig pieces in my pocket and of course – the box. If I wanted to I could sell it. Those two crooks were in that line of business. Their pockets were simply bursting with watches, rings, and jewellery. Their wallets were stuffed with notes. They pounced on anything shiny, just like magpies.

Elisa pushed the frankfurters over the counter. They lay hot on cardboard plates, with a slice of bread and a dollop of mustard.

'Here you are, boys,' she said.

Wasinski put both sausages into his mouth at once. He disgusted me.

'Well, not hungry?' he asked.

'Yes.'

'If it's for the money, you can come along now.'

'No, I can't.'

'Why not?'

'No, I just can't! Not now, anyway; not this moment.'

'O.K.,' said Wasinski, 'you can come later. Let's say, at eleven. At eleven near the taxis, right?'

'O.K., at eleven near the taxis.'

I bit into my second sausage. Wasinski looked me up and down.

Ich faßte nach meiner Brusttasche. Da war die Kapsel und zeichnete sich ab im Stoff der Tasche.

«Also gut, um elf bei den Taxis.» Er zahlte und ging.

Die Rumänen oder Ungarn redeten noch immer aufeinander ein. Elisa zerknüllte die Kartons und warf sie unter die Theke.

Ich sagte: «Gib mir noch Zigaretten. Vier Stück. Zu mehr reicht es nicht.»

«Brüder seid ihr!» kreischte sie wieder und zählte vier Zigaretten aus der Packung. Ich wollte Zeit gewinnen, zwei, drei Minuten, bis Wasinski fort war.

Aus der Bar nebenan hörte man die Tanzmusik. Vor dem Eingang stand Brigitte, die kleine, schwächliche Brigitte, die mir immer leid tat, wenn ich sie mit einem Amerikaner sah. Gern wäre ich öfter mit ihr zusammen gewesen, doch sie nahm mich nicht ernst. Jetzt stand sie allein drüben. Ich ging vorbei. Ich tat, als sehe ich sie nicht. Sie rief: «Hallo! Hallo!» Zwei-, dreimal. Ich ging weiter, als höre ich sie nicht. Ihre klopfenden Absätze liefen über den Asphalt, kamen näher, holten mich ein. Sie packte mich am Arm und drehte mich auf der Stelle um.

«Hörst du nicht mehr?»

Ich tat erstaunt: «Brigitte, wie geht's?»

«Danke, ich warte mal wieder,» sagte sie.

«Und es lohnt sich?»

«Das stellt sich später heraus. Mein William ist nochmals nach oben, ich habe meine Puderdose liegen lassen, aber ich weiß nicht mehr genau, in welchem Lokal. Das ist das dritte, in dem wir suchen. Wenn sie da nicht ist, kann sie mir gestohlen bleiben.»

«Puderdose brauchst du nicht.»

«Soll das ein Kompliment sein?»

«Vielleicht.»

«Weißt du was», sagte sie unvermittelt, «du gehst mit

I felt for my breast pocket. The box was there, its outline visible in the material of the pocket.

'Right then, at eleven near the taxis,' he said, and went out.

The Rumanians or Hungarians were still chattering. Elisa crumpled the cardboard plates and threw them under the counter.

I said: 'Let me have some cigarettes. I want four fags – can't afford any more.'

'You are a fine lot,' she yelled again, and counted out four cigarettes from the packet. I just wanted to gain time, two, three minutes, till Wasinski had gone.

From the bar next door came the sound of jazz. Brigitte stood at the entrance. Little, fragile Brigitte for whom I always felt sorry when I saw her with an American. I wouldn't have minded seeing a bit more of her, but she did not take me seriously. Now she was there alone. I went by. I pretended not to see her. She called 'Hey there! Hey there!' Twice, three times. I went on as if I had not heard. The staccato sound of her heels on the pavement came closer, caught up with me. She gripped me by the arm and pulled me round on the spot.

'Can't you hear any more?'

I feigned surprise. 'Brigitte, how are you?'

'Thanks, I'm on the wait again,' she said.

'And is it worth while?'

'That we must see later. William has just gone upstairs again. I've lost my powder-compact somewhere, but I can't remember where. This is the third place we are trying. If it isn't here it can go hang for all I care.'

'You don't need a powder compact.'

'Is that a compliment?'

'Could be.'

'You know what,' she said suddenly, 'you come up

mir nach oben. Du tanzt mit mir, und bei der Gelegenheit kann ich sehen, ob William – »

«Nein, das geht nicht. Ich habe keine Zeit. Wasinski wartet.»

«Ach, der!»

Sie zog mich an der Hand unter den Eingang, die schmutzige Holzstiege hoch. Auf dem Parkett drängten sich die Tänzer, ganz eng. Die Kapelle spielte einen Boogie-Woogie.

«O, Boogie!» stieß Brigitte hervor.

«Ja, Boogie!» Mir fuhr der Rhythmus in die Glieder. Ich verdiente mir manchmal das Essen mit Tanzen. Der Wirt gab mir an Abenden, wenn nicht viel los war, freie Zeche[7] und nach Mitternacht in der Küche ein Rumpsteak, wenn ich nur dablieb, engagierte und tanzte. Ich habe ganze Nächte durchtanzt, mit Frauen, die mir gleichgültig waren. Nun tanzte ich mit Brigitte. Ich vergaß die Hostie. Alles vergißt man beim Tanz. Die Kreppsohlen treten die Widerstände nieder. Auch Brigitte tanzte gut. Ihr Gesicht glühte. Ich riß sie an mich.

«Was hast du da?»

«Wo? Was?»

Ihre Hand fuhr nach meiner Brusttasche: «Hier!»

«Nichts!»

«Gib sie her, du Schuft!»[8]

«Was denn, Brigitte, ich weiß ja gar nicht – »

«Das ist meine Puderdose, du Schuft, du gemeiner, dreckiger Schuft!»

Sie wollte die Tasche aufreißen. Der Knopf sprang ab. Ich stieß sie weg und drängte zur Tür.

Brigitte schrie: «Haltet ihn! Dieb! Dieb!»

Sie fielen über mich her. Wie roh sie sein konnten, die Kavaliere, die Leisetreter mit den seidenen Hemden, den bunten Socken und den Gabardinehosen. Sie traten mir in

with me. We'll dance, and while we're there I can look
around and see if William –'

'Sorry, can't be done. I haven't got time. Wasinski is
waiting.'

'Oh, him.'

She pulled me by the hand into the doorway, up the
dirty wooden staircase. The floor was crowded with
dancers, all quite close to one another. The band played
a boogie-woogie.

'Oh, boogie!' Brigitte exclaimed.

'Yes, boogie.' I felt the catching rhythm. Dancing
sometimes earned me a meal. On those evenings when
there weren't many people around, the publican allowed
me drinks on the house and a rump steak in the kitchen
after midnight provided I stayed and asked the girls to
dance. I have danced all night long with women who
didn't mean anything to me. Now I danced with
Brigitte. I forgot about the host. You forget about
things when you dance. Crêpe soles crush all resistance.
And Brigitte danced well. Her face was glowing. I
pulled her close to me.

'What have you got there?'

'Where? What?'

Her hand felt my breast pocket: 'Here.'

'Nothing!'

'Give it to me, you bastard.'

'What's up, Brigitte, I don't know what . . .'

'That is my compact, you bastard, you mean, dirty
bastard!'

She wanted to tear open the pocket. The button came
off. I pushed her away and made for the door.

Brigitte yelled: 'Stop him. Thief, thief!'

They fell upon me. Those gents and sneaks with their
silk shirts, their coloured socks and gaberdine trousers,

die Hüfte, schlugen mir ins Gesicht. Ich wehrte mich, so gut es ging, ohne meine linke Hand von der Brusttasche zu lassen. Zwei Burschen waren da, die zu mir halfen. Auch Wasinski kam dazu. Wir boxten uns zum Ausgang.

Auf der Straße fragte Wasinski: «Was machst du für Geschichten?»

«Eifersucht,» sagte ich, «pure Eifersucht.»

«Du bist schön dumm.»

«Saudumm.»

«Weißt du übrigens, wie spät es ist?»

«Keine Ahnung.»

«Elf Uhr. Ich hatte dich bestellt, nicht wahr?»

«Ich sagte dir doch – »

«Du mußt dich entscheiden: entweder so'n Mensch oder einen Job.»

«Ich geh ja mit.»

Wir gingen das rechte Trottoir hinunter bis zur Kneipe[9] der Taxichauffeure. Ihre Autos standen vor dem Eingang. Sie selber standen drinnen in ihren Lederjacken und Trenchcoats. Hinter dem Büfett das speckige Gesicht von Blaschke. An einem der Tische vor den geschlossenen Vorhängen saßen Pschorrn, Kremer, und Richard.

Pschorrn sagte: «Ihr bequemt euch auch, zu kommen.»

Kremer sagte: «Die Herren!»

Richard sagte: «Du blutest ja.»

Ich sagte: «Kleinen Zwischenfall gehabt – wegen Weiber.» Das war plausibel für sie. Wir setzten uns, Richard schob mir seine Packung Lucky Strike über den Tisch, Pschorrn beugte sich zu Wasinski und tuschelte ihm ins Ohr.

Die Chauffeure waren sehr vergnügt. Auch der, den sie «Lohengrin» nannten, ein versackter Opernsänger, war da.[10] Wenn er betrunken war, erinnerte er sich seiner früheren Erfolge. Er hob das Glas und sang mit schmel-

how savage they could be! They kicked me in the side, hit me in the face. I defended myself as well as I could without taking my left hand from my breast pocket. There were two fellows who came to my aid, then Wasinski joined in. We managed to fight our way out.

In the street Wasinski asked: 'What are you up to?'

'Jealousy,' I said, 'pure jealousy.'

'You are pretty silly.'

'Bloody silly.'

'You know, by the way, what time it is?'

'No idea.'

'It's eleven o'clock. I told you to be there, remember?'

'But I told you –'

'You must make up your mind: either that kind of tart or a job.'

'All right, I'm coming.'

We walked down on the right side of the road to the taxi-drivers' joint. Their cabs were waiting outside. The drivers in their macintoshes and leather jackets were inside, Blaschke's greasy face behind the counter. At one of the tables near the drawn curtains sat Pschorrn, Kremer, and Richard.

Pschorrn said: 'Well, well, turning up at last.'

Kremer said: 'Ah, the gentlemen!'

Richard said: 'But you've blood on your face.'

I said: 'Had a small incident – women, you know.' That made sense to them. We sat down, Richard pushed his packet of Lucky Strikes across the table. Pschorrn leaned over to Wasinski and whispered into his ear.

The drivers were very merry. The one whom they called 'Lohengrin', a one-time opera-singer who had gone off the rails, was there too. Whenever he was drunk he would remember his former triumphs. He would raise his glass and sing in a melting falsetto: 'In a

zender Kopfstimme: «In fernem Land, unnahbar euren Schritten, liegt eine Burg, die Monsalvat genannt – » Er sang nicht schlecht. Man wurde gepackt davon, ob man wollte oder nicht. Es wurde ruhiger in der Kneipe; seine Kollegen spreizten den Daumen und sagten zu fremden Gästen: «Lohengrin!» Er sang immer nur den einen Satz, brach ab und schüttete einen Schnaps nach. Manchmal kam es vor, daß einer rief: «Sing was Gescheites! Einen Schlager!» Dann blies er die Backen auf, stieß die Luft aus und sagte: «Bäh, einen ordinären Schlager. Lo-hen-grin! Wissen Sie, was das ist? Ich sang den Lo-hen-grin: in Zürich, in Elberfeld, in Meiningen, in Kiel!» und seine Worte gingen über in Gesang: «In fernem Land – »

«Mensch, hör hierher!» Wasinski stieß mir in die Seite. Pschorrn sagte: «Ihr beide übernehmt die Ware und bringt sie in die Albrechtstraße, weiter nichts. Ihr macht ein Dutzend kleine Packen daraus, dann habt ihr sechsmal zu gehen. Klappt die Geschichte, wiederholen wir morgen. Kapiert?»

«Ja», sagte Wasinski.

«Du auch?» fragte er mich.

«Ja», sagte ich, obwohl ich nicht wußte, um was es ging und was in den Paketen transportiert werden sollte. Wasinski hatte zwei Bier bestellt. Wir tranken leer und gingen aus der Kneipe. Als wir unter der Tür im Freien standen, kamen vier oder fünf Autos die Straße vom Bahnhof herunter. Es waren diese klotzigen, milchweißen Wagen der Militärpolizei. Wasinski hielt mich am Ärmel, stutzte und sagte: «Hau ab.» Da lief er auch schon. Auch ich lief, in entgegengesetzter Richtung, so schnell ich konnte. Wasinski lief zu den Trümmern, ich lief die Straße hinunter, um nicht den gleichen Weg zu haben. Ich sah mich nicht um, ich lief, ich lief. Ich griff nach der Brusttasche und fühlte

far-away land, inaccessible to men, there lies a castle, Monsalvat by name.' He did not sing badly. One couldn't help being gripped by it, whether one liked it or not. The noise stopped; his colleagues would point their thumbs at him and inform strangers among the customers: 'Lohengrin!' He would never sing more than that one sentence, break off, and pour a *Schnaps* down after it. Occasionally, it happened that somebody called out to him: 'Why don't you sing something nice! A hit tune!' Then he would blow up his cheeks, puff out the air and say: 'Pah, you and your vulgar tunes. Lo-hen-grin! Do you know what that means? I sang the Lo-hen-grin–in Zürich, Elberfeld, Meiningen, Kiel!' and he would fall into singing again: 'In a far-away land –'

'Man, listen here!' Wasinski nudged me. Pschorrn said: 'You two take over the goods and take them to Albrecht Street, and that's that. Make up a dozen small packages; that means you'll have to go six times. If the thing works, we'll do it again tomorrow. Got it?'

'Yes,' said Wasinski.

'What about you?' he asked me.

'Yes,' said I, although I had no idea what it was all about and what was inside the packets which we were to carry. Wasinski had ordered two beers. We drank up and left the place. As we stood in the doorway outside, four or five cars were coming down the street from the station. They were those heavy milk-white patrol cars of the military police. Wasinski grabbed me by the sleeve, drew himself back, and said: 'Beat it!' And off he was. I also ran, in the opposite direction, as fast as I could. Wasinski made for the bomb site. I raced down the street. I did not turn round, just ran. I put my hand

die Kapsel. Ich lief um meine Freiheit, ich lief, die Hostie zu retten.

Sie waren hinter mir her. Die Sirene heulte. Die Straße teilte sich in zwei Straßen, die ein Rondell[11] umschlossen. Auf dem Rondell stand eine Kirche, hohe, graue Mauern, mit dem schwarzen Loch eines Portals. Ich sprang über die Straße. Der Kühler streifte mich fast, doch ich entkam ins Portal.

Die Kirche war zerstört. Vier Mauern, darüber der Nachthimmel. Ich stolperte über Steine, stieß an Blöcke und Säulen, stürzte in eine Grube. Die Strahlen ihrer Taschenlampen kreuzten sich über mir. Ihre Stimmen riefen: «Stehenbleiben! Stehenbleiben!» Es widerhallte. Mein Kinn war aufgerissen. Blut tropfte in den Halsausschnitt. Schnell nahm ich die Kapsel aus der Tasche und schob sie unter einen Stein. Dann gab ich auf.

Sie zerrten mich herauf und setzten mich in eines ihrer Autos. Wir fuhren zur Taxikneipe. Sie war umstellt. Ein Menschenknäuel. Bekannte waren darunter, Pschorrn, Kremer, Richard. Wasinski nicht. Sie lieferten uns im Revier XIV ab, und das Verhör begann, ein langweiliges, uninteressantes Verhör. Die Polizisten tranken Kaffee aus dicken Porzellantassen. Sie packten Brötchen aus und strichen Leberwurst darauf.

Wenn ich freikomme, dachte ich, dann mache ich Schluß und beginne von vorn. Aber ich wußte auch, wie lange solche Vorsätze anhielten.

Ich kam frei. Warum, weiß ich nicht. Ihre Fragen und meine Antworten waren so gewesen, daß ich nicht erwartete, freigelassen zu werden.

«Sie können gehen,» sagte der Polizeirat.

«Wohin?» wollte ich fragen, aber ich fragte nicht und ging rasch zur Tür. Die andern schwiegen, nur Richard rief nach: «Mach's gut!»

to my breast pocket and felt the box. I ran for my freedom, I ran to save the host.

They came after me. The siren screamed. The street divided into two crescents enclosing a church in the centre, with tall grey walls and the black hole of a porch. I leapt across the road. The car radiator almost caught me, but I escaped into the porch.

The church was in ruins. Four walls, above them the night sky. I stumbled over stones, bumped into blocks and pillars, fell into a trench. The beams of their electric torches crossed on top of me. Voices cried: 'Stand still! Stand still!' It echoed. I had cut my chin. Blood dripped down my neck into my open collar. Quickly I took out the box from my pocket and pushed it under a stone. Then I gave myself up.

They pulled me out and put me in one of their cars. We drove back to the taxi-drivers' joint. It was surrounded by police. A throng of people, some familiar faces, Pschorrn, Kremer, Richard, but not Wasinski. We were taken to police station 14 where the questioning started, a dull, uninteresting questioning. The policemen were drinking coffee from thick china cups. They unwrapped rolls and spread liver sausage on them.

If I get off, I thought, I'll finish with this and start again. But I also knew that resolutions like that usually didn't last very long.

I did get off. Why, I don't know. After their questions and my answers I had not expected to be released.

'You may go,' said the police inspector.

I wanted to ask him, 'Where?', but didn't, and went quickly to the door. The others were silent, only Richard called after me: 'All the best!'

«Du auch.»

Ich ging aus dem Gebäude, die Treppe hinab, auf die Straße. Es war ein Sonntagmorgen. Wenige Autos fuhren. Die Straßenbahnen waren fast leer. Der Himmel war blau, klar, kühl. Ich hätte mich gern gewaschen, rasiert, die Schuhe geputzt, aber ich wollte nicht zur Schlafstelle zurück. Zuerst mußte ich die Kirche wiederfinden. Ich ging zur Florinstraße, von dort wußte ich den Weg.

Ich ging an der Taxikneipe vorbei. Das Rondell kam, die Kirche. Bei Tag war es gleich zu erkennen, daß sie zerstört war. Ich holte die Kapsel aus der Grube, stieg heraus, und hinter der Kirche ging ich weiter in ein Viertel, in dem ich noch nie gewesen war. Eine schwarzgekleidete Frau mit einem Stock und einem Pekineserhündchen kam daher. Ich fragte nach einer Kirche, nach einer, die nicht zerstört sei.

«Oh, Sie wußten nicht, daß St Johannis zerstört ist?»

«Nein, ich wußte es nicht.»

«Ach, Sie sind fremd.»

«Ja, ich bin fremd.»

«Und eben erst angekommen?»

«Ja, eben.»

Sie musterte mich von Kopf bis Fuß und sagte: «Passen Sie auf: Sie gehen diese Straße einfach weiter, bis zur vierten Querstraße nach rechts,[12] und dann – was machst du, Fifi? – dann gehen Sie noch etwa zweihundert Meter geradeaus, und Sie stehen direkt – kommst du her, Fifi?–»

Ich sagte «danke» um ihre Erklärungen abzubrechen. Sie faßte mich am Ärmel und sagte: «Sie können es nicht übersehen. Man sieht die Kirche schon von weitem. Es ist die Kirche vom Heiligsten Herzen Jesu.»

Sie formte den Mund zu einer Röhre, wenn sie sprach. Rasch ging ich weg. Rechts und links lagen Wohnhäuser mit Gärten davor. Lackierte Gattertüren mit Emaille- und Messingschildern. Die Namen von Direktoren und ameri-

'Same to you.'

I went out of the building, down the steps, into the road. It was Sunday morning. Few cars were about. The trams were almost empty. The sky was blue, clear, and cool. I could have done with a wash and a shave, my shoes needed cleaning, but I did not want to go back to my lodgings. First I had to find the church again. I walked to Florin Street as I knew my way from there.

I passed the taximen's joint. There was the crescent, the church. In daylight one could see at once that it was a ruin. I fetched the little box from the trench, climbed out again and continued walking on behind the church, into a part of the town I had never been to before. A woman dressed in black with a walking-stick and a tiny Pekinese dog came towards me. I asked for the nearest church, one that was not destroyed.

'So you did not know that St John's was bombed?'

'No, I didn't know.'

'Then you're a stranger here.'

'Yes, I am a stranger.'

'And just arrived?'

'Yes, just.'

She examined me all over and said: 'Look, you simply go along this street, and take the fourth turning to the right and then – what are you doing, Fifi? – another two hundred metres and there it is in front – Fifi, come here!'

I said 'thanks' to stop further explanations. She held my sleeve and said: 'You can't miss it. The church can be seen from far away. It is the Church of the Most Sacred Heart of Jesus.'

Her mouth formed into a tube when she spoke. Quickly I went on. To the right and to the left there were villas with front gardens. Varnished gates of fencing with enamel and brass-plates. Names of direc-

kanischen Offizieren. «Achtung vor dem Hund» und «Beware of the dog».

Die vierte Querstraße rechts kam. Ich bog um die Ecke und sah die Kirche. Ihre Fassade riegelte die Straße ab.

Als ich die Stufen hochstieg, öffneten sich oben die Türen. Die Orgel dröhnte einen Choral, und es war, als drücke er die Menschen, die in der Kirche waren, heraus. Eine Prozession. Voraus gingen Mädchen in weißen Kleidern, die Haare offen. Ihre Händchen griffen in kleine Körbe und streuten Rosenblätter und die Blütenköpfe von Margueriten und Kornblumen, Jungen folgten den Mädchen, in blauen Anzügen, mit Auslegekragen, einen Scheitel durch das wassernasse Haar gezogen. Eine Schar Nonnen, die Köpfe geneigt. Eine Gruppe Mönche. Der Chor kam, Männer und Frauen, die die Melodie der Orgel in voller Harmonie mitsangen. Die Meßbuben, in roten Röcken und spitzendurchbrochenen Hemden, schwangen – wie ich einmal – die goldenen Fässer, aus denen Weihrauch stieg. Ein Baldachin füllte das Portal. Die Seide war bestickt mit Edelsteinen. Der Wind bauschte die Seide. Darunter gingen drei Priester, der in der Mitte trug die Monstranz. In einem Bündel goldener Strahlen, in einen silbernen Halbmond gesetzt, die Hostie.

Ich kniete nieder, obgleich ich nicht wollte. Die Prozession zog an mir vorbei. Sie sangen, beteten, murmelten. Schuhe traten mich. Ellenbogen stießen. Mäntel und Gehröcke voller Mottengeruch streiften mich.

Ich haßte diese Prozession. Die da vorbeigingen, hatten nichts mit mir zu tun. Sie waren so ruhig, ich so unruhig. Sie waren mir fremd mit ihren Singsang, ihren verdrehten Augen, ihrer eingelernten Frömmigkeit. Wie aus dem Polizeirevier ging ich auch hier weg, um allein zu sein. War ich allein? Ich hatte die Hostie. Ich nahm sie mit in mein unruhiges Leben.

tors and American officers. Notices: '*Achtung vor dem Hund*' and 'Beware of the dog'.

There was the fourth turning. I turned the corner and saw the church. Its massive front blocked the street.

As I went up the steps, the church doors opened. The organ boomed a hymn, and this seemed to have the effect of driving out the people who were inside the church. A procession was forming up. In front, girls in white dresses, with long hair. Hands went into little baskets and strewed rose petals and the blooms of marguerites and cornflowers. Boys followed the girls, in blue suits, their open-neck shirt collars turned outwards, a parting drawn through hair that had been damped with plenty of water. A flock of nuns with their heads bowed. A group of monks. Then came the choir, men and women, joining their voices harmoniously to the organ melody. Altar-servers in red cassocks and linen tunics trimmed with lace were – as I had done once – swinging golden vessels which emitted clouds of incense. Now a canopy filled the porch. The silk was embroidered with precious stones. The wind swelled out the silk. Underneath, three priests were walking, the one in the middle carried the monstrance. In a bundle of golden rays, set in a silver half-moon – the host.

Against my will I knelt down. The procession passed by. They chanted, prayed, mumbled. Shoes trod on me, elbows pushed, coats and jackets smelling of moth-balls brushed me.

I hated this procession. Those who went past were strangers to me. They were so calm, I was so restless. They meant nothing to me with their chanting, their oblique gaze and studied piety. I left the place, as I had the police station, in order to be by myself. But was I really alone? I had the host. I took it away with me into my restless life.

WOMAN DRIVER
GERTRUD FUSSENEGGER

Translated by Patrick Bridgwater

DAME AM STEUER

Es ist ja nicht wahr, was Fedja immer sagt, ich habe den Teufel im Leib, sobald ich am Volant sitze. Zugegeben, ich fahre rasch, rasch, aber sauber.[1] Kann man denn sauber fahren, wenn man rasch fährt?

Der Abend – aufgeklart nach Regen. Im Westen, fern, der blaßgelbe Schein, der Himmel reingefegt und kalt wie aus Jade. Die Stadt sinkt unter der Rampe weg. Wie kühn die Straße steigt, Kurve um Kurve. Da unten in dem Lichtgesprenkel blinkt auch Fedjas Haus und das meine. Er sitzt daheim[2] und liest, liest und denkt nach und schweigt, die Uhr tickt, ihre Zeiger kriechen, von Zeit zu Zeit stäubt Fedja seine Zigarette ab und die Asche häuft sich in der Schale.

Da – im Rückspiegel, was ist das? großer breitgedrückter bronzebrauner Ball – ah, der Mond! geht dort im Osten auf, schweres glosendes[3] Licht, Mond im September. Man nennt ihn Jägermond, wohl weil September die Zeit der Jäger ist, Halali über Heide und Felder, die Büchse knallt und das Wild birgt sich zitternd im Busch.

Was willst du, altes Gestirn, dein Schein ist nichtig, nichtig geworden in unseren Nächten, die hell sind von anderen und so viel stärkeren Lichtern. Bist nicht mehr fern wie einst, unerreichbar, alter Mond der Liebenden, Freund der seufzenden Dichter. Das Geschoß[4] hat dich getroffen, eine Wunde deiner eisigen Haut geschlagen, deiner narbigen Kraterhaut. Erst gestern hab ich mit Fedja darüber geredet, und Fedja sagte: Wozu das alles? Ich verstehe die Menschen nicht. – Und ich darauf: Fedja,

WOMAN DRIVER

IT's simply not true, as Fedja always maintains, that the devil's within me the moment I'm sitting behind the wheel. Admittedly I drive fast; fast, but well. Is it possible to drive well if one is driving fast?

The evening – clear after rain. In the west, far away, the pale yellow light, the sky swept clean and looking as cold as jade. The town is falling away now behind the slope. How boldly the road is climbing, curve after curve. Down there among the speckles of light, Fedja's house and mine is blinking away. He's sitting at home reading, reading and thinking and not saying a word, the clock is ticking away, its fingers are creeping round, from time to time Fedja flicks the ash off his cigarette and the ash will be mounting in the ash-tray.

There – in the rear-mirror, what's that? A great flat-looking bronze-brown ball – ah, the moon! Rises in the east, a dull, gleaming light, the September moon. They call it the Hunter's Moon, because September is the huntsman's season I suppose, 'Tally-ho!' over moors and fields, the gun barks, and the deer hides trembling with fear in the wood.

What do you want, poor old star, your light is nothing, is nothing now in our nights which are bright with other and far stronger lights. You are no longer remote as you were once, no longer beyond our reach, old moon of lovers, friend of sighing poets. The rocket struck you, cut a wound in your icy skin, in your skin pock-marked with craters. Only yesterday I was talking

verstehst du denn auch nur mich? – Da machte er die Augen schmal und schaute mich lange an und sagte endlich: Nicht immer, Barbara, verstehe ich dich.

Nicht immer? Nie verstehst du mich, Fedja; am wenigsten, wenn ich abends wegfahre ohne Ziel und Zweck, fahre wie jetzt, nur um den Wagen zu steuern, um nicht mit dir im Zimmer zu sitzen, wo die Uhr tickt, wo sich die Schale mit Asche füllt, wo dein Schweigen die Wände anschweigt[5] daß sie näher rücken, immer näher, bis mir ist, als würden sie mich erdrücken.

Da muß ich fahren, Fedja. An Ausreden fehlt es mir nicht, wenn du sie mir auch nicht mehr glaubst, diese armseligen Lügen. Auch heute belog ich dich: Ich wollte Ruth besuchen, meine Schwester, die krank ist. Ja, krank ist sie; trotzdem besuch ich sie nicht, und du weißt es, weißt, daß ich Ruth nicht mag, daß ich im Grunde niemand mag, nicht einmal – dich.

Ah, Ortschaft! Aufgepaßt! Hier wird die Straße eng, verdammt! wie ich die Engen doch hasse, vollgestopft mit Radfahrern, Fußgängern, Kindern und Hunden. Finster und ungeschlacht biegt ein Fuhrwerk ums Eck,[6] Ackergäule, ein Fuder Heu – sollte verboten sein auf einer Straße wie dieser!

Mein guter Wagen, hab Geduld, mein guter schöner Wagen, nur Geduld, gleich sind wir draußen, gleich bist du wieder frei. Da – endlich: open drive. Häuser und Menschen bleiben zurück, die Straße stürzt uns entgegen und der Wind, der süße sausende Ton, der an den Scheiben zerblättert.[7] Schneller! Schneller! Der weiße Streifen rennt uns voraus, die roten Zwinkeraugen an den Randsteinkappen, schneller, schneller fliegen Signale vorbei: Kreuzung, Kurve, Gefälle. Immer rufen die Tafeln: Gefahr! Gefahr! Wer möchte denn fahren ohne Gefährdung?

Was uns entgegenkommt: weggezischt wie ein spuk-

to Fedja about it, and Fedja said: What's the point of it all? I don't understand human beings. And I in reply: Fedja, do you even understand me? He narrowed his eyes and looked at me for a long time, and finally said: I don't always understand you, Barbara.

Not always? You've never understood me, Fedja; least of all when I drive off in the evening without rhyme or reason, drive like I'm driving now, just for the sake of steering the car, to avoid sitting with you in the room, where the clock is ticking away, the ash-tray filling with ash, where your silence is a silent appeal to the walls, so that they close in, close in more and more, till I feel as though they are going to smother me.

Then I *have to* go driving, Fedja. I'm not short of other excuses if you don't believe them any longer, these pitiful lies. I lied to you again today, saying I wanted to visit Ruth, my sister, who's ill. She's ill, all right; but all the same, I don't visit her, and you know it, know that I can't stand Ruth, that I really can't stand anyone, not even – you.

Ah, built-up area! Look out! The road's getting narrow here, damn! How I hate these narrow roads, chock-full with cyclists, pedestrians, children, and dogs. Dark and ponderous, some sort of vehicle is turning the corner, cart-horses, a cartload of hay – ought to be banned on a road like this!

Old car, be patient, my beautiful old car, be patient, we'll be out of it soon, soon you'll be free again. There it is now at last – clearway. Houses and people are being left behind, the road is tearing towards us and the wind, the sweet sighing sound sweeping its leaves against the windows. Faster! Faster! The white line is running ahead of us, the red cat's-eyes on the kerb-stones, faster and faster the signs flash past: Cross-Roads, Bend, Steep

haftes Bild. Was vorne ist: eingeholt, überholt, aus-
gelöscht ins Irgendwo-hinter-uns. (Soll keiner glauben, er
fahre schneller als ich, soll keiner glauben: nur eine Dame
am Steuer!) Wärest du jetzt neben mir, Fedja, du fingest
zu wettern an: Bist du verrückt? – Über Hundert! – Aber
du bist nicht da, sitzest daheim in der Stube, blätterst in
deinen Büchern, spinnst[8] an Erinnerungen oder an Plänen
für später. Plan und Erinnerung, ein und dasselbe Netz,
das uns das Leben einfangen soll, Leben, wie du es meinst.
Immer und Einerlei. Aber ich will es nicht, dieses gefangene
Leben. Ich will das Jetzt und Hier, dieses Hier, das schon
Dort ist, open drive soweit der Scheinwerfer reicht, Halali
auf der Straße, Jagd und Beute. Was ist die Beute einer
solchen Nacht?

Früher jagten die Jäger zu Pferd. Die Büchse knallte: ein
Knäuel Pelz und zuckendes Fleisch, verglaste Augen,
milchig und blicklos, nachher die dampfende Mahlzeit,
und das war alles. Heute jagt man zu Wagen.[9] Die Beute:
Schein und Chimäre, Ritt auf dem Rücken des Lichts,
weißen Scheinwerferkegels, ins Rußschwarz der Nacht
geschleudert, weißer Kahlschlag des Lichts quer durch die
Finsternis. Fließband der Landschaft, Wald und Fels wie
Kulissen, spulen[10] heran und vorbei, Brücken, Mauern,
Geländer – irgendwo brüllt ein Gießbach, irgendwo tobt
ein Abgrund, aus phantomhafter Schlucht weht eine
Wasserfahne, farblos stiebender Schaum.

Alle Dinge entwest[11] zu farblos stiebendem Schaum.

Ja, es ist wahr, was Fedja einmal mir sagte: Liebe ist nicht
in dir, nur die Gier nach dem Nichts.

Ja, es ist wahr, ist wahr. – Aber was ist dieses Nichts?

Hat es nicht auch ein Gesicht? Unser eignes Gesicht?
Nein. Es ist anders und fremd, unerreichbar und schön.

Neulich – wie war das doch – auf einer Fahrt wie dieser,
oder träumte ich sie? Ja, ich träumte sie nur, diese Fahrt

Hill. Always the signposts call out: Danger! Danger! Who would want to drive but for the sense of danger?

Everything coming towards us goes swishing past like a ghostly apparition. Everything ahead of us is caught up, overtaken, obliterated to somewhere-behind-us. (Let none of them think he can drive faster than me, let none of them think: only a woman driver!) If you were beside me now, Fedja, you would be starting to curse: Are you crazy? – Over a hundred! – But you're not there, you're sitting at home in the room, turning the pages of your books, spinning a crazy web of memories or plans for later. Plan and memory: one and the same web designed to snare our life, life as you understand it. But I don't want it, this life-in-a-snare. I want the here-and-now, this here which is already there, clearway as far as the headlamps reach, tally-ho on the road, hunt and quarry. What is the quarry for a night such as this?

Time was when huntsmen hunted on horseback. The gun barked: a ball of fur and quivering flesh, glazed eyes, milky and unseeing, afterwards the meal served piping hot, and that was all. Now we hunt mounted on cars. The quarry: phantom and chimera, riding mounted on lights, on the white cone of the headlamps, hurtling into the soot-black of night, a white clearing of light slicing its way through the dark. Conveyor-belt of scenery, woods and rocks like backdrops, come reeling towards us and past, bridges, walls, railings – somewhere a mountain torrent is raging, somewhere an abyss is roaring, out of some ghastly chasm a trail of water is blown, spray colourless in the air.

All things dissolve into spray colourless in the air.

Yes, it's true, what Fedja said to me once: There is no love in you, only a yearning for the void.

ins Gebirge und, wie Träume schon sind: alles war groß
und phantastisch, riesig die Landschaft, riesig die Nacht,
und die Straße, immer hinauf, hinauf, endlos, spiralig,
schwindelnde Viadukte übereinander getürmt. Vor mir ein
blauer Wagen. Marke? Mir unbekannt. Aus einem fremden
Land wohl, Fremdling auf meiner Straße, immer vor mir,
schneller und immer noch schneller, unüberholbar, wie
ich mich auch beeile. Sollte er mir entfliehen? Nein, ich
will ihn erreichen. Angst, daß er mir entschwinde, Angst,
weil die Straße so schmal wird, immer engere Kreise zieht
sie auf immer engeren Kurven, und der Fremdling – kein
Wagen – öffnet die silbernen Flügel, lächelt aus blauem
Visier ...

Da ist die Straße verschwunden – Bodenloses verschlingt
mich.

Über den Straßenrand führt eine Reifenspur, und ein
junger Mann, der von der Arbeit heimfährt, spät, auf dem
Rad, hat sie entdeckt und gemeldet.

Am nächsten Morgen eine Notiz in der Zeitung: Der
tägliche Tod auf der Straße und so weiter.

Immer so weiter unter dem Jägermond.

Yes, it's true, true. But what is this void?

Does it not have a face? Is its face not our own? No. It is other than us and strange, out of our reach and beautiful.

Recently – how did it come about – when driving like this, or did I dream it? Yes, I dreamt it merely, this drive up into the mountains; and, as dreams always are, everything was larger than life and fantastic, giant scenery, giant-like the night, and the road, ever upwards, upwards, endless, spiralling, giddy viaducts towering one over the other. In front of me a blue car. Make? Not one I know. From some foreign country, I suppose, a foreigner on my road, keeping in front of me all the time, faster and faster still, going too fast to be overtaken, however hard I keep my foot down. Is he going to get away? No, I'll catch him, I will. Afraid that he may elude me, afraid because the road is getting so narrow, sweeping in tighter and tighter circles round ever narrower bends, and the stranger – not a car at all – opens his silvery wings, smiles from behind his blue visor. . . .

Now the road has vanished into thin air – bottomless space is swallowing me up.

Over the edge of the road a tyre mark, and a young man travelling home from work, late, on his bicycle, has found and reported it.

The following morning a report in the paper: The death-a-day on the road and so on.

And so on for ever under the Hunter's Moon.

ANTIGONE AND THE
GARDEN DWARF

GERD GAISER

Translated by Dieter Pevsner

ANTIGONE UND DER GARTENZWERG

DÄMONEN?[1] sagte der alte Herr am Tisch: traut man euren Autoren, so ist diese Erde ihre Domäne, eine Dämonen-Domäne, verwaltet von Leviathanen, durchstreift von Satansboten, bevölkert von Managern, Robotern, und Funktionären. Andere Modelle werden nicht anerkannt. Dem Gartenzwerg etwa, obwohl er eine Lebensmacht ist, wird so gut wie keine Beachtung geschenkt.

Richtig, sagte Joachim, unser Freund, der Pfeife rauchte. Dabei gewinnt der Gartenzwerg jetzt mit der zunehmenden Bautätigkeit täglich an Boden.

Denn nichts, fuhr der alte Herr fort, entbehrt der Mensch schwerer als seinen Gartenzwerg, seinen Dämon ausgenommen. Zuweilen wird sogar der Gartenzwerg zum Dämon –

Wozu ich, unterbrach ihn Silvia, unsere Freundin, eine Geschichte beibringen kann –

Einen Augenblick noch! oder der Dämon zum Gartenzwerg. Seht etwa die Aszendenz des Gartenzwergs an: jeder weiß, Moritz von Schwind ist sein beschämter Vater.[2] Und der bezog seine heroischen Gnomen von den Riesen des Michelangelo. Der Gartenzwerg ist eine Stilphase. Es gibt kaum etwas, das nicht zum Gartenzwerg werden könnte.

Ich bin ein simpler Mensch, sagte Joachim wieder, aber mir gibt es der Traum manchmal ein. Hört, ich träumte, und da war ein ungeheurer, verrauchter, nach oben verdämmernder Raum, ein Zelt, eine Riesenscheune, und

ANTIGONE AND THE GARDEN DWARF

'DEMONS?' said the old man sitting at the table. 'If authors are anything to go by, the world is their domain, a demons' domain administered by Leviathans, travelled by messengers of Satan, and populated by managers, robots, and civil servants. No other brands allowed. Ornamental garden dwarfs, for example, are as good as ignored, even though they are an important force in the world.'

'Quite right,' said our friend Joachim, who was smoking his pipe. 'Although the garden dwarf is gaining ground almost daily nowadays, what with the increased amount of building going on.'

'For there is nothing that Man finds it harder to do without than his garden dwarf,' continued the old man, 'except his Demon. In fact there are times when garden dwarfs become demons . . .'

'Which reminds me,' our friend Silvia interrupted, 'I've got a story about that.'

'Just a minute . . . or demons become garden dwarfs. Look at the ancestry of the garden dwarf. We all know that its father was, to his shame, Moritz von Schwind, who derived his heroic gnomes from Michelangelo's giants. The garden dwarf is a stylistic phase. Hardly anything that exists is incapable of becoming a garden dwarf.'

'I'm just a simple chap,' said Joachim, 'but I'm some-times inspired in my dreams. Listen. I once dreamt I saw an enormous smoky hall, rising up into blackness like a

eine Menge, von Untergangsängsten geschüttelt, hockte und wogte darin. Aus Lautsprechern fallen schrecklich deformierte Stimmen und künden den Dämon an. Niemand weiß, wer das ist, endlich ein schriller, gräßlich gezogener Schrei, dann ein Plärren: er ist da, der Namenlose, niemand wagt es, ihn anzusehen. Auf dem Podeste rast er, dann tobt er den Gang herunter durchs Auditorium. Die Menge keucht, alle Gesichter preßt die Angst an den Boden. Da stößt jemand mich sachte an, das kennt ihr vielleicht, das findige und ironische zweite Ich im Traum: Sieh's dir doch an, sagt es. Und wie ich so schiele, was da am Wüten ist, fange ich an zu lachen: es ist ein Vorgartenzwerg, einer mit Bartkrause und dümmlichen, hellblauen Augen. Und schon ist er wie eine Gasflamme weg.[3]

O je, Gartenzwerge, sagte Silvia jetzt, unsere Freundin, die Gärtnerin. Sie glauben nicht, was Gartenzwerge für ein Artikel sind. Ein Geschäft kann nicht genug davon führen, und Sie brauchen sich nicht einmal mit den Preisen in acht zu nehmen. Jeder Gartenzwerg geht weg. Passen Sie auf: einmal nachmittags, draußen regnet es, muß ich im Laden, wo die Blumen verkauft werden, Dienst machen.[4] Ein Mensch kommt herein, ein Herr, der den Schirm zusammenklappt. Einer von den angenehmen Kunden, die sich durchs Fenster entschließen. Gleich faßt er die Ecke ins Auge, wo unsere Zwerge stehen, und deutet auf unseren teuersten, den wir haben, einen von der großen Sorte, stehend, mit Pfeife im Mund. «Den, Fräulein,» sagt er und hat noch nicht einmal nach dem Preis gefragt.

«Schön,» sage ich, «bitte sehr», und wackle auf der Stehleiter, denn das Ding wiegt etwas: «Achtunddreißig achtzig käme der.» – Der Herr hat dagegen nichts, hat aber das ganze Geld nicht bei sich, so gibt er zwanzig

tent or a gigantic barn, with a crowd crouching and heaving in it, shaking with eschatological terror. Horribly distorted voices issue from loud-speakers, heralding the Demon. Nobody knows who it will be, but at last there is a shrill, hideously drawn-out scream, then a blubbering sound: the nameless one has arrived, nobody dares look at him. He rages on the dais, then tears down the gangway through the auditorium. The crowd gasps, their faces pressed to the floor in fear. At that moment somebody gives me a gentle nudge (you probably know that ubiquitous, ironic second self that exists in dreams). 'Why don't you look at it?' it says. And when I squint up to see what it is that's raging, I burst out laughing. It is a front-garden dwarf, one of those with a short curly beard and stupid pale-blue eyes. Then it's gone, like a gas flame.'

'Oh my goodness, garden dwarfs,' said our friend Silvia, the gardener. 'You can't imagine what they're like as a selling line. You can't stock too many of them in a shop, and you don't even need to be careful about prices. Every garden dwarf goes. Listen. One afternoon it was raining outside and I had to serve in the shop where we sell our flowers. A man came in, a gentleman closing his umbrella – one of those ideal customers who make up their minds through the window. He looked straight at the corner where we keep our dwarfs and pointed at the most expensive one we had, one of those big ones with a pipe in its mouth. "That one, Miss," he said, without even asking the price.

'"Very good, Sir. Thank you very much," I said, wobbling on the step-ladder under the weight of the thing. "This one is thirty-eight marks eighty." The gentleman didn't mind, but he hadn't enough money on him, so he paid twenty marks deposit and made quite

Anzahlung und paßt genau auf, daß ihm der Zwerg zurückgestellt wird. Endlich geht er, und da steht jetzt der Zwerg und wartet.

Jetzt paßt einmal auf, was kommt. Eben wollen wir schließen, da stürzt noch ein Mensch in den Laden, ein Mensch mit so einem geschwollenen jähzornigen[5] Gesicht, der hat sich draußen auch schon vor den Scheiben herumgebückt, jetzt geht er geradewegs auf den Gartenzwerg los, der doch verkauft ist, und faßt ihn an und sagt: «Den, Fräulein. Ich nehme ihn sofort mit, Fräulein.»

«Oh,» sage ich, «das ist aber schade», und ich fürchte mich ein bißchen, denn der Mann hat so etwas Merkwürdiges in seinem jähzornigen geschwollenen Gesicht, so etwas von einem Süchtigen oder Amokläufer. «Wirklich ganz außerordentlich bedauerlich,» sage ich, «aber das Stück ist fest verkauft. Erst vor einer Stunde ist es verkauft worden.» «Das kann nicht sein,» schreit der Mensch jetzt und ist schon in Wallung. Er hat einen Hut auf wie ein Jäger, sieht aber sonst eher aus wie einer, der sich im Büro aufregt: «So hat es nicht kommen dürfen, so nicht!» «Wir werden versuchen, ihn wieder hereinzubringen. Ich gebe die Bestellung.» «Unmöglich!» und der Mensch rückt hinter mir her und mir auf den Leib und schreit flüsternd: «Wissen Sie auch, daß es sich um den Wunsch einer sterbenden Frau handelt? Nein? Sie liegt im Sterben! Und dazu haben wir jetzt gebaut! In der Wielandstraße, Fräulein, mit einem Vorgarten, und bloß auf den Zwerg haben wir noch gespart. Und haben es uns ausgedacht, Fräulein, alles, wie er sein muß und wo er stehen soll, so, daß eines[6] ihn immer sieht, wenn es durchs Fenster guckt. Und jetzt soll sie ihn nicht mehr kriegen? Ich lasse sie nicht sterben, Fräulein, eh sie nicht noch durchs Fenster den Zwerg hat stehen sehen. Da ist mir alles egal.»

Er steht, starrt mich an, fuchtelt und fistelt,[7] und ich,

sure that the dwarf was put on one side for him. Finally he left, and the dwarf stood and waited.

'Now listen what happened next. When we were just about to close, another man, who had also been craning his neck outside the window, rushed into the shop – a man with one of those swollen, apoplectic faces. He marched straight up to the garden dwarf I had just sold, took hold of it, and said, "This one, Miss. I'll take it with me, Miss."

'"Oh, I'm sorry," I said, a little frightened because the man had an extraordinary look about his swollen, apoplectic face, the look of a maniac or a man who might run amok. "I'm terribly sorry," I said. "This one is sold. It was sold just an hour ago." "It can't have been!" the man shouted, coming to the boil at once. He was wearing a hunting hat, but apart from that he looked more like one of those men who get their excitement at the office. "This should never have happened. No, not this!" "We'll try and get another one in. I'll order one for you." "Impossible!" The man followed close on my heels, shouting, in a stage whisper, "Do you realize this is a dying woman's request? No? She's at death's door! We've built ourselves a special house, in the Wielandstrasse, Miss, with a front garden, and the only thing we still had to save up for was this dwarf. We had it all worked out, Miss, what it was to be like, and where it was to stand so that you would always be able to see it when you looked out of the window. And now you say she's not to have him? I won't let her die, Miss, before she's seen that dwarf through the window. I don't care what you say."

'He stood staring at me and gesticulating, so what could I do? I couldn't just do nothing. "I could ask

was soll ich tun? Dabei kann ich nicht gleichgültig bleiben.[8]
Man könnte die Chefin fragen, denke ich, aber gleich sage
ich mir: Ach was, Chefin. Antigone hätte in so einem Fall
auch nicht die Chefin gefragt. – Und ich renne und helfe
ihm einpacken, damit er noch recht kommt, und werfe das
Geld in die Kasse und halte ihm noch die Tür. Erst wie er
fort ist und ich das Gitter herunterlasse, wird mir wieder
schwummerig, aber dann sage ich mir noch einmal, und
das stärkt mich: Antigone hätte genauso gehandelt.

Was kommt? Man hätte sich einigen können, aber es
geht nicht gut ab. Am andern Tag kracht es im Laden,
und ich werde herbeigeholt, und die Chefin hat einen roten
Kopf, und der Käufer, dem der Gartenzwerg ja gehört,
droht mit den Gerichten. Er will durchaus nicht seine
zwanzig Mark zurückhaben, auch keine Bestellung
abwarten, und die Frau, die im Sterben liegt, macht gar
keinen Eindruck auf ihn. Er ist schrecklicher in seinem
Starrsinn als der andere gestern in seiner Verzweiflung:
er will seinen Zwerg haben. «Außerordentlich peinlich,»
sagt die Chefin, und: «Sie müssen Ihr Recht bekommen.»
Und zu mir sagt sie unfreundlich: «Stellen Sie es an, wie
Sie wollen, aber stecken Sie Geld ein und sehen Sie zu,
daß Sie den Artikel wieder beibringen.» «Ich will es
versuchen,» sage ich zerknirscht.

Wie ich den Mantel anziehe, ist mir nicht heldinnen-
mäßig zumute. Das hast du jetzt, denke ich bei mir, von
deiner alten Antigone. Immerhin, denke ich weiter, wenn
das stimmt mit der Wielandstraße und dem Vorgarten,
ist es nicht ganz unmöglich. Und es könnte doch sein, daß
die Frau vielleicht inzwischen – nun ja, daß der Zwerg
inzwischen, sozusagen, wieder frei geworden ist. «Und
ich,» ruft der Kunde, der wie ein Schießhund aufpaßt,
«werde mich Ihnen anschließen. Ich begleite Sie.»

Die Straßenbahn fährt ja die ganze Wielandstraße

the manageress," I thought, but then I said to myself, "Antigone wouldn't have asked the manageress in a case like this." So I ran to help him pack it, to make sure he got home in time, threw the money into the till, and even held the door open for him. I didn't get nervous again until after he'd gone and I was letting down the grille, and then I gave myself courage by telling myself, "Antigone would have done the same."

'What happened? Well, we could have reached some kind of agreement, but the story doesn't end happily. The next day there was a racket in the shop. I was fetched. The manageress was looking red-faced, and the customer who really owned the garden dwarf was threatening to go to court. He adamantly refused to take back his twenty marks, or to wait for another to be ordered, and the woman at death's door didn't impress him in the least. His obstinacy was worse than the previous day's man's despair: he wanted his dwarf. "Most embarrassing," said the manageress, and, "You must certainly have what's yours in law." Then she turned crossly to me: "I don't care how you do it, but take some money and make sure you get the article back." "I'll try," I said, contritely.

'I didn't feel very heroic as I put on my coat. "It was your old Antigone landed you in this," I thought. "Still," I continued to myself, "if what he said about the Wielandstrasse and the front garden is true, it shouldn't be impossible. And perhaps by now his wife is . . . well, maybe the dwarf is, as you might say, available again." "As for me," shouted the customer, who had been watching me like a pointer dog, "I shall join you. I shall accompany you."

'The tram goes all along the Wielandstrasse, so there I stood on the platform, with the man behind me

entlang, und ich stehe auf der Plattform mit dem Menschen hinter mir, der wie ein Schießhund aufpaßt, und dem Geld in der Manteltasche. Die Gegend ist neu, lauter sauber zusammengesparte Häuschen, und schon fängt es an mit den Gartenzwergen hinter den Zäunen. Plötzlich sehen wir dann sehr viele Gartenzwerge auf einem Haufen, und da ist unser großer drunter, man sieht ihn auf den ersten Blick, und wir schreien uns aufgeregt an auf der Plattform: «Da ist er», daß die Leute uns merkwürdig angucken. An der nächsten Haltestelle stürzen wir los. Ich bitte den Menschen: «Ach, bleiben Sie doch vielleicht erst einmal ein bißchen zurück.»

Der Gartenzwerg stand da also, und nicht allein, er glotzte aus einer ganzen Versammlung von stehenden, liegenden, kauernden oder hopsenden Gartenzwergen oder solchen, die sich hinter dem Ohr kratzten. Aber er fiel auf, es war, das mußte man zugeben, ein prächtiges Exemplar seiner Gattung. Unter den Kerlen richtet sich jetzt übrigens eine Frau auf, eine ziemlich starke Frau mit einer Küchen- schürze und einer Brille, sie hat eben Suppengrün[9] ab- geschnitten und kann also nicht die sein, die im Sterben liegt. Hat sie aber gestern noch im Sterben gelegen und ist sie es, so haben wir da ein Wunder. Ich fasse mir ein Herz, und ich steige hinauf, stottere und sage öfters: Verzeihung, und daß alles so peinlich sei. Sie begreift aber nicht viel von meinen Reden, fängt an, mich nachsichtig anzuschauen aus ihrer Höhe, denn so ganz stimmt es da nicht, und erst, wie ich anfange: «es handelt sich nämlich, verstehen Sie, um einen Mann, der im Sterben liegt» wird sie gleich gutmütig, sagt: «Der da? Ja, den hat er gestern gebracht. Aber regen Sie sich doch nicht so schrecklich auf, Fräulein.» Und sie zieht den Kerl aus dem Boden wie eine Rübe, die starke und großmächtige Person: «Wenn das so ist, Fräulein, nehmen sie ihn ruhig wieder mit.»

watching like a pointer dog, and the money in my pocket. It was a new district, with lots of clean, painfully saved-for little houses. Almost immediately the garden dwarfs began behind the fences. Suddenly we saw a large number of garden dwarfs in a crowd, with our big one immediately recognizable among them. "There it is!" we screamed excitedly at one another on the platform, and the other passengers looked at us oddly. At the next stop we leaped off, and I asked the man, "Won't you stay behind a little, just to start with?"

'So there he was, our garden dwarf, and not alone either. He glared at us from among a whole assembly of garden dwarfs, standing, lying, crouching, jumping, some of them even scratching behind their ears. But he caught your eye. He was, one had to admit, a splendid specimen of his kind. At that moment a woman rose from among the assembly – a fairly powerful woman, wearing a kitchen apron and spectacles. As she had just been cutting herbs for soup, she could hardly be the one at death's door. Or if she was the one, and had been at death's door the day before, then we were witnessing a miracle. Taking courage, I walked up to her, stammered, and said several times that I was sorry and how embarrassing it all was. But she couldn't understand what I was talking about, and at first looked down suspiciously at me, thinking that something was not quite right. But when I started saying, "Well, you see, it's connected with a man at death's door," she immediately turned friendly and said, "Oh, that one? Yes, he brought that one yesterday. Don't get so het up, Miss." And, being the powerful woman she was, she pulled the little fellow out of the ground like a turnip. "If that's how it is, Miss, you're welcome to take it away again."

Und sie stutzt, die Person, wie ich ihr die Achtunddreißig achtzig in die Hand drücke, sieht sich das Geld an
und lacht: «Sie dürfen wiederkommen, wenn Sie noch
einmal einen brauchen oder wenn jemand stirbt, Fräulein.»
Und sie lacht noch eine Weile hinter mir her, ganz tief
wie ein Mann. Da begreife ich langsam: Das ist gar nicht
die Frau. Der Mann sammelt Gartenzwerge.[10]

Aber jetzt schnell, denke ich, renne und habe den
Greuel auf dem Arm, und der Vitzliputz[11] grinst und wiegt
ziemlich viel, und hinter mir muß die Frau immer noch
lachen. Schon stürzt auch mein Beschützer vor, der Mann,
der auf mich aufpaßt, er nimmt mir den Kerl ab und
trägt ihn, und wir rennen weiter. Hoffentlich kommt jetzt
gleich die Elektrische, denke ich bei mir, als wir bei der
Haltestelle angelangt sind und beide schnaufen. Hoffentlich kommt sie schnell, und dann wird es noch gut! Und
die Elektrische kommt, trotzdem wird es leider nun nicht
gut, denn es ist die falsche Elektrische oder vielmehr die
aus der falschen Richtung, sie kommt von der Stadt her.
Wer steigt aus und sieht uns drei mit einem Blick, wie wir
dastehen, der Zwerg, der fremde Mensch, und dabei ich?
Sie brauchen sich nicht viel zu besinnen, und verwunderlich
ist dabei nichts, denn schließlich ist es ja seine Haltestelle.

Also er sieht uns, und von der Schwelle des Wagens
nimmt er uns an[12] mit seinem grünen Hut und seinem
geschwollenen jähzornigen Gesicht, er springt auf den
Mann los, der den Gartenzwerg auf dem Arm hat, mit
einem Satz wie ein Tiger. Und ich sehe eben noch, wie der
andere Mann den Zwerg vorsichtig wegsetzt, ehe sie sich
anfassen, damit dem Zwerg nichts passieren kann, und
sehe noch mit dem letzten Blick, wie der Dämon an die
Hecke gelehnt ist und sein Maul sich verzieht zu einem
greulichen Grinsen.

Aber wieso letzter Blick? rufen wir aus einem Munde.

'When I pressed the thirty-eight marks eighty into her hand she was taken aback, looked at the money, and laughed. "You can come again, Miss, if you ever need another one, or if somebody dies." And she went on laughing for some time as I left, in a deep voice like a man's. Then it slowly dawned on me: it wasn't his wife. The man collected garden dwarfs.

'"But now I'd better be quick," I thought, so I ran, with the monster lying heavy on my arm grinning at me, the little devil, while behind me the woman still couldn't stop laughing. My protector, the man watching me, appeared immediately, relieved me of the dwarf, and we ran on together. "I hope the tram comes soon," I thought when we reached the stop, both of us panting. "I only hope it comes soon, so that we can have a happy ending!" The tram did come, but unfortunately we didn't have our happy ending because it was the wrong tram, or rather it was going the wrong way – coming from town, that is. And who should get off and with his very first glance see the three of us standing there, the dwarf, a strange man, and me? You won't need to think very hard. In fact it wasn't really all that surprising; after all, it was his own tram stop.

'So he saw us, and from the very step of the tram-car closed on us with his green hat and his swollen, apoplectic face. He leaped like a tiger at the man with the garden dwarf on his arm. I just saw the other man stand the dwarf carefully to one side to make sure nothing happened to it, before they came to grips. And with my very last glance I saw the Demon leaning against the hedge, with his mouth contorted in a hideous grin.'

'But why your last glance?' we cried in unison.

Ja, denn ich hielt es nicht aus, mir war so schwach in den Knien, und da sprang ich vorn auf den Wagen, als der anfuhr, und fuhr mit dem Wagen weit fort bis zur Endstation.

Und dann?

Sie müssen sich zerrissen haben. Und dann fuhr der Dämon häßlich meckernd[13] mit ihnen zur Hölle.

Aber woher wissen Sie das?

Die Elektrische fuhr weit hinaus bis dorthin, wo sie mit einer Schleife kehrt macht, und ich fuhr die Schleife mit und blieb im Wagen sitzen, bis er wieder zurückfuhr. Wir kamen dort wieder vorbei an jener Haltestelle, und da war nichts mehr zu sehen von allen dreien. Merken Sie es jetzt? Von allen den dreien kein Fäserchen mehr.

Ja, aber wie ist das mit dem Geld geworden, Silvia?[14]

Mit welchem Geld, ruft Silvia erschrocken.

Jetzt hatten Sie doch wieder Geld zu kriegen. Achtzehn achzig von Ihrem ersten Kunden.

Lieber Schreck, sagt Silvia kläglich. Ja, im Geschäft tauge ich wenig.[15] Es ist klar, und ich hatte daran noch nicht einmal gedacht. Es war tatsächlich ein Dämon.

'Well, I couldn't stand it, my knees went so weak. So I jumped into the front of the tram as it moved off, and rode all the way to the terminus.'

'And then?'

'They must have torn each other to pieces. After which the Demon went down to Hell with them, bleating horribly.'

'But how do you know?'

'Well, the tram went all the way out to where it turns round in a loop, and I rode round the loop, then waited in the car until it started back again. We came past the stop once more, and there was no trace of any of the three. Now do you understand? Not the smallest trace of any of them.'

'Yes. But what happened to the money, Silvia?'

'What money?' cried Silvia, startled.

'Surely you were owed some more money. Eighteen marks eighty. By your first customer.'

'Holy Moses!' said Silvia plaintively. 'I never was much of a business woman. It's so obvious, but it never even occurred to me. It must have been a Demon.'

AT THE TROCADERO

WOLFDIETRICH SCHNURRE

Translated by John Cowan

UND dann rissen sie die Tür auf und warfen mich raus. Ich fiel hin und blieb einen Augenblick liegen, denn die Kühle des Pflasters tat gut, wenn man die Stirne draufdrückte. Dann stand ich auf und ging langsam zum Bahnhof.

Der letzte Zug war aber schon weg; da setzte ich mich ins Bistro und aß eine Wurst. Ich hatte vor, ins Trocadero zurückzugehen; nicht, weil ich denen noch eine reinhauen wollte, ich wollte nur sehen, was mit Wittigkeit war. Aber ich war zu betrunken; ich schlief ein und bin eben erst aufgewacht.

Es ist Morgen, die Stühle stehen auf den Tischen, es riecht nach Fleischbrühe, Bohnerwachs und nach Kaffee, auf den Karosserien der Autos tänzelt die Sonne, und man hört den Zeitungsverkäufer die Frühblätter ausrufen.

Ich muß immer noch an Wittigkeit denken. Es war idiotisch von mir, daß ich ihn ansprach. Aber was soll man machen, Wittigkeit ist so was wie ein Stück Jugend gewesen, und ich dachte doch immer, das wäre alles flöten gegangen[1] im Krieg; und da sehe ich ihn nun gestern nacht an dieser Baustelle im Scheinwerferlicht stehen und seine Blechflasche auskippen. Nur die Maurerkluft[2] störte ein bißchen, sonst sah er genau so aus wie damals, als er vor seinen achthundert Schafen herging, alle halbe Stunde einen Schritt, und Augen, so abwesend, daß nichts in ihren Blicken hängenzubleiben schien. Im Dorf sagten sie immer, er hätte das Zweite Gesicht; aber daß er vorausgesagt hatte, das Forsthaus brennt ab, das lag

AT THE TROCADERO

AND then they tore open the door and threw me out. I went full length and lay there for a while; it felt good to press one's forehead against the cool stones of the pavement. Then I got up and walked slowly to the station.

However, the last train had already gone; so I sat down in a bistro and ate a sausage. I intended to go back to the Trocadero; not that I wanted to pitch into them again – I just wanted to see what had happened to Wittigkeit. But I was too drunk; I fell asleep and have just this minute woken up.

It is morning; the chairs have been put on the tables; there is a smell of meat-soup, floor-polish, and coffee; the sun is shimmering on the coachwork of the cars, and I can hear the newspaper-boys selling the early editions.

I still keep on thinking of Wittigkeit. It was stupid of me to speak to him. But what is one to do? Wittigkeit has always been something like a part of my boyhood to me, a boyhood I had for long thought of as gone for good in the war; and suddenly last night I see him on this building-site standing in the light of the arc-lamps and tipping out the contents of his tin flask. Apart from the bricklayer's rig-out, which looked a bit odd on him, he was exactly the same as when he used to walk along in front of his eight hundred sheep, one step every half-hour or so and such a far-away look in his eyes that they never seemed to focus on anything. They used to say in the village that he had second sight; but the reason why he had been able to predict that the forester's house

daran, er ist es selber gewesen, der es angesteckt hat, er mochte dem Förster den Tod seines Hundes nicht verzeihen. Dabei war der Förster im Recht, denn Ajax hatte gewildert; doch das kümmerte Wittigkeit nicht; er hat in Ajax seinen Bruder gesehen, und einen Brudermord rächt man. Ich wartete, bis er die Klotzpantinen[3] mit den Schuhen vertauscht hatte und sich seine Joppe anzog und die Mütze aufsetzte. «Tag, Wittigkeit,» sagte ich dann.

Auch er erkannte mich gleich; doch nichts in seinem Gesicht bewegte sich; alles blieb ausdruckslos, glatt und verschlossen.

«Wie geht es dir?» fragte ich.

«Nu –» sagte er, «wie schon.»

Wir liefen ein Stück zusammen und redeten von den Wäldern bei Deutsch Krone und dem Dorf Stibbe, Kreis Schneidemühl,[4] wo Wittigkeit her war. Nach den Schafen allerdings getraute ich mich nicht zu fragen, es war was in seinem Gesicht, das es einem verbot.

Nach einer Weile kamen uns die anderen entgegen, ich hatte sie völlig vergessen; seit ich an der Baustelle stehengeblieben war, hatte ich nur noch den Geruch von Wittigkeits Schafherde im Kopf und das hechelnde[5] Belfern der Hütehunde und den Ton der Holunderflöte, mit der er sich die Zeit vertrieb.

«Was ist 'n los?» fragte Leo, «willste nicht mehr?»

«Ich hab 'n Bekannten getroffen,» sagte ich.

«Ah –» machte Budd und sah Wittigkeit an.

Wittigkeit räusperte sich und rückte an seiner Mütze.

«Das ist Herr Wittigkeit,» sagte ich; «ich kenn ihn von früher.»

Sie gaben ihm alle die Hand.

«Sie kommen doch mit, Herr Wittigkeit?» fragte Vinka. Sie blinzelte zu Budd hin, und Budd griente[6] und sagte:

would burn down was simply that he was the one who
set it on fire; he was not prepared to forgive the forester
for causing the death of his dog. And actually the forester
had been in the right, for Ajax had been destroying
game; but Wittigkeit hadn't worried about that; Ajax
had been a brother to him, and for the murder of a
brother one takes revenge. I waited until he had changed
from his wooden slippers into a pair of shoes and put on
his jacket and cap. Then I said, 'Hello, Wittigkeit.'

He recognized me immediately too; but he did not
move a muscle; his face remained expressionless, smooth
and hard.

'How are things with you?' I asked.

'Oh, well,' he said with a shrug, 'as you might expect.'

We walked on for a bit together and talked of the
forests by Deutsch Krone and the village of Stibbe in the
parish of Schneidemühl where Wittigkeit came from.
But I did not dare ask him about his sheep, for there was
something in his face that forbade one to do so.

After a while the others came towards us; I had completely forgotten them; since stopping at the building-site I had thought of nothing but the smell of
Wittigkeit's herd of sheep, the staccato bark of the
dogs, and the sound of the elderwood-flute which
he used to play to pass the time.

'What's up?' Leo asked. 'Don't want to come with
us now?'

'I've met a friend,' I said.

'Oh –' said Budd, and looked at Wittigkeit.

Wittigkeit cleared his throat and tugged at his cap.

'This is Herr Wittigkeit,' I said. 'I know him from
the old days.'

They all shook hands with him.

'I hope you'll join us, Herr Wittigkeit?' Vinka asked.

«Leo hier, der hat sich nämlich von Astrid getrennt, wissen Sie, und das feiern wir heute.»

Wittigkeit stand zwischen ihnen, die Leuchtreklame vom Rouge baiser und gegenüber die vom Pelikanfüller überzogen sein ausdrucksloses Gesicht mal mit Rot, mal mit Blau; er räusperte sich, man merkte, er wollte gern weg, und ich wollte auch, daß er ginge, aber da hakten ihn Budd und Leo schon unter, Vinka klopfte ihm lachend auf die Schulter, und sie zogen ihn mit.

Jedes Frühjahr wurden die Schafe immer geschoren, und die Wolle wurde in Säcke gepackt und ins Gutshaus gebracht. Die Wolle war fettig und mit Staub, Laub und mit Kot verklebt, man mußte sie erst tagelang waschen, ehe sie gebleicht werden konnte. Die Schafe waren während dieser Zeit in zwei Buchten gesperrt. In der einen Bucht waren die ungeschorenen, in der anderen die geschorenen Tiere. Die Ungeschorenen sahen dick und schwerfällig aus. Die Geschorenen waren mager und sprangen herum, sie freuten sich, daß sie auf einmal so leicht waren. Dann war noch eine kleinere Bucht da, in die wurden die Tiere gesperrt, die kastriert werden sollten. Das besorgte Wittigkeit selbst; er brauchte nicht mal einen Gehilfen dazu, und er war berühmt für die Art, wie er es machte. Die kastrierten Schafe standen alle auf einem Haufen; sie ließen die Köpfe hängen und rührten sich nicht; es dauerte oft Wochen, bis sie wieder Freude hatten am Leben.

Leo hatte im Trocadero einen Tisch bestellt; er stand dicht an der Tanzfläche, wir hatten Mühe, uns durch die Paare hindurch zu ihm hinzuarbeiten.

Wittigkeit war nicht zu bewegen gewesen, Joppe und Mütze abzugeben, und er hatte ja wohl auch noch seine Maurerkluft drunter. Jetzt hatte er die Hände in die schrägen Taschen der Joppe geschoben und besah sich mit seinem ausdruckslosen Gesicht das Lokal; die Mütze hatte

She shot a glance at Budd, who grinned broadly and said: 'Fact is, Leo here has just left Astrid and we are going to celebrate.'

Wittigkeit stood between them; the neon lighting of the *Rouge baiser* advertisement and the one for Pelikan fountain pens opposite flooded his expressionless face red one minute, blue the next. He cleared his throat and one could see that he wanted to leave – and I wanted him to go – but Budd and Leo put their arms through his, one on each side of him; Vinka patted him on the shoulder, and they drew him along.

The sheep were always shorn in the spring; and the wool was stuffed into sacks and brought to the estate-house. The wool was greasy and plastered together with dust, leaves, and droppings; it had to be washed for days before it could be bleached. During this time the sheep were enclosed in two pens. One for the unshorn, the other for the shorn. The unshorn looked fat and clumsy. The shorn were thin, and jumped about, happy to feel suddenly so light. Then there was another smaller pen in which the sheep that were to be castrated were shut. Wittigkeit always dealt with this himself; he did not even need an assistant to help him, and he was famous for the way he did it. The castrated sheep huddled close together; they hung their heads and kept quite still; often it took weeks for them to regain their former *joie de vivre*.

Leo had ordered a table at the Trocadero; it was right up next to the dance-floor, and we had a job working our way towards it through the dancing couples.

We hadn't been able to persuade Wittigkeit to leave his jacket and cap with the cloakroom attendant – he was probably still wearing his bricklayer's get-up underneath. He had shoved his hands into the slanted pockets of his jacket and was taking a look at the club, his face

er über sein Knie gestülpt,[7] er saß genau so da, wie er im Winter immer in der Dorfkneipe in Stibbe gesessen hatte, nur der Schafgeruch fehlte.

Es waren eine Menge Bekannte von uns da. Rechts saß Vistral, der Catcher; neben ihm saßen Lore und Giska, die Schauspielerinnen hatten werden wollen, aber Nutten geworden waren. Dahinter saß Herbert, der Eintänzer, mit seinen Jungen; und dann war noch Mäxi, der Dichter, da mit einem Haufen Verehrerinnen um sich herum, alles Backfische und Akademiedohlen;[8] und auch Rachmiel, der desertierte Russe, war da und noch ein paar.

Sonst waren hauptsächlich junge Männer mit bleichen Stirnen und großen Brillen da und Mädchen mit glänzenden Nasen, sie sahen aus wie ungelüftete Betten. Alle tanzten mit ernsten Gesichtern, denn es standen nur Coca-flaschen mit Strohhalmen drin auf den Tischen; die Sekt-trinker hatten sich ins Dunkle verkrochen, sie wollten nicht, daß man sie sähe.

Die Kapelle war gut, besonders der Schlagzeuger. Er war dünn und bestand fast nur aus Röhrenhosen und Rhythmus, und hätte man ihm das Schlagzeug weggenommen, er hätte noch tagelang weitergezuckt und -gezappelt, dann wäre er hingestürzt und gestorben.

Wir fingen mit Beaujolais an, dann gingen wir über zu Mosel, und dazwischen wurde Pernod, Whisky, und Wodka getrunken. Wittigkeit wollte erst nicht; aber schließlich schaffte Vinka es doch, ihn rumzukriegen, und er nahm seine Hand aus der Tasche und prostete uns zu und hielt mit.

Am aufregendsten war es immer gewesen, wenn die Schafe im März das erste Mal wieder rauskamen. Sie sprangen und rannten dann wie die Wahnsinnigen, keines dachte an Fressen, sie zogen los, als wollten sie alle Weide-plätze der Welt erobern und legten ein Tempo vor, daß

as usual expressionless. He had put his cap over his knee and sat there just as he used to sit in the village pub at Stibbe in wintertime; the only thing that was missing was the smell of the sheep.

Quite a few friends of ours were there. On our right was Vistral the wrestler, and sitting beside him Lore and Giska, who had wanted to be actresses, but who had become tarts. Behind them sat Herbert the gigolo, with his young men; and then there was Mäxi the poet, surrounded by a swarm of his female fans, all of whom were teenagers and beatnik types from the Art School; Rachmiel the Russian deserter was there too, and a few more.

Otherwise most of the people present were young men with pale foreheads and large spectacles and girls with shiny noses; they looked like beds that hadn't been aired. They were all dancing with serious expressions on their faces, as the only drinks on the tables were Coke-bottles with straws; the champagne drinkers had crept off into the dark to avoid being seen.

The band was good, particularly the chap on drums. He was skinny, and made up of drainpipe-trousers, rhythm, and little else; if the drums had been taken away from him he would have gone on twitching convulsively for days before falling down dead.

We started off with Beaujolais, switched over to Moselle, and drank Pernod, whisky, and vodka in between. Wittigkeit didn't want to drink anything at first; but Vinka finally succeeded in persuading him; he took his hand out of his pocket, drank our health, and joined in.

The most exciting moment of all was always in March when the sheep were let out for the first time. They jumped and ran around like mad things; they scampered off with no thought of food as if they wanted to conquer all the pasture-lands in the world, and struck

manchmal sogar die Hütehunde abgehängt wurden. Es
dauerte Wochen, ehe Wittigkeit sie so weit zur Raison
gebracht hatte, daß sie sich Zeit nahmen beim Äsen und
einsahen, der Sinn ihres Lebens lag nicht im Rennen, er
lag in der Ruhe. Meist ließ Wittigkeit sie um den Großen
Böthiensee herum weiden. Da gab es den Seeadler noch;
die Wasserfläche wurde rings vom Land angefressen, und
nur im Vorfrühling, wenn die Schneeschmelze ihn stärkte,
konnte der See einen Gegenschlag wagen; doch nicht
lange, und seine Schlenken[9] wurden wieder zum Rückzug
gezwungen und Erlen, Schilffelder und Heere von Binsenkubben[10] stießen nach und schoben sich immer weiter in
den Seespiegel vor. Das Gras hier war pelzig und zart, es
schmeckte wie Sahnebonbons, wenn man drauf kaute, und
die Schafe waren noch verrückter nach ihm als nach Salz.

Je mehr Wittigkeit trank, desto redseliger wurde er. Das
war neu an ihm; in der Dorfkneipe früher hatte er nur in
sein Bierglas gestarrt und geschwiegen. Er erzählte vom
Bau und was er vorher gemacht hatte. Er hatte Teppiche
geklopft, Kohlenkähne entladen, «und einmal», sagte er,
«hab ich bei 'ner Ingenieursfrau gewohnt, und ich hab ihr 's
Badezimmer gekachelt und ihr 'n Holzschuppen gebaut.»

«'ne neuerungssüchtige Dame,» feixte Vinka.

«Sie war gut,» sagte Wittigkeit; «und sie stammte aus
Schneidemühl, wissen Sie.»

Alle lachten, und Wittigkeit fuhr sich mit dem Hand-
rücken über den Mund und erzählte weiter, was er so alles
gemacht hatte. Er sprach immer lauter; von den anderen
Tischen sahen sie schon zu uns rüber und stießen sich an
und machten sich über Wittigkeit lustig.

Auch Leo und Budd amüsierten sich sehr, und Vinka
kam aus der scheinheiligen Fragerei gar nicht mehr raus;
sie war so in Fahrt, daß sie nicht mal merkte, wie ich sie
anstieß.

up such a speed that sometimes even the dogs were left behind. It was weeks before Wittigkeit was able to calm them down sufficiently for them to take time over their grazing and to realize that the whole point of their life was not in racing but in rest. Generally Wittigkeit used to let them graze on the edge of Lake Böthien. In those days there were still white-tailed eagles to be seen; the surface of the water was eaten into all around by the land; it was only in the early spring, when the melting snow strengthened the lake, that it dared to hit back, but it wasn't very long before its mobile columns were compelled to retreat and alders, belts of reed, and armies of black-headed gulls followed up the attack and thrust themselves farther and farther into the waters of the lake. The grass here was downy and tender; it tasted like cream caramels when it was chewed, and the sheep were crazier for it than they were for salt.

The more Wittigkeit drank, the more talkative he became. This was something new in him; in the old days in the village pub he had merely sat there in silence staring into his beer glass. He talked about building work and what he had done before. He had beaten carpets, unloaded coal-lighters, 'and once,' he said, 'I stayed with the wife of an engineer and tiled her bathroom and built her a wood-shed.'

'She must have been a great one for making changes,' said Vinka with a giggle.

'She was a kind woman,' said Wittigkeit; 'and she came from Schneidemühl, you know.'

They all laughed and Wittigkeit drew the back of his hand across his mouth and went on telling about all the things he had done. He spoke more and more loudly; at the other tables they were already looking over at us, nudging each other and making fun of Wittigkeit.

Ich betrank mich schneller, als ich es mir vorgenommen hatte; ich war wütend auf sie; sie hatten kein Recht, sich über Wittigkeit lustig zu machen, niemand hatte dazu ein Recht. Wittigkeit war zwanzig Jahre lang Gutsschäfer gewesen, und zuletzt hatte seine Herde über achthundert Köpfe gezählt. Er konnte Böcke kastrieren und Muttertieren Geburtshilfe leisten. Er konnte aus dem nassesten Holz Feuer anmachen und aus dem Schnepfenstrich die Beschaffenheit des kommenden Sommers ablesen. Er konnte ein gebrochenes Schafbein schienen, daß es in zwei Wochen wieder zusammengewachsen war, und er verstand Flöten zu schnitzen, mit denen man den Pirol und den Wiedehopf anlocken konnte: Niemand hatte ein Recht, sich über ihn lustig zu machen; hier nicht und nirgendwo.

Aber sie taten es alle, das ganze Lokal amüsierte sich jetzt über ihn. Er merkte es nicht. Er saß da in seiner mörtelstaubgepuderten Joppe, seinem schmuddeligen Kunstseidenschal, die Mütze über dem Knie, in der einen Hand das Glas, die andere hatte er Vinka auf die Schulter gelegt, und redete und redete, und trank und redete.

«Und zuletzt,» sagte er, «da haben sie die ganze Herde zusammengeschossen; sie sollte den Russen nicht in die Hände fallen, hieß es. Sie stellten MGs um den Kral auf und hielten dazwischen, zuerst fielen bloß immer ein paar um, aber dann, als sie nicht mehr ganz so dicht standen, wurden es mehr. Sie brachen immer erst in den Vorderbeinen zusammen, die Hinterbeine blieben noch stehen.

Dann legten sie den Kopf auf die Seite, und dann fiel auch das Hinterteil um. Schließlich war bloß noch der Leithammel übrig. Er hatte schon x-mal was abgekriegt und ganz rote Augen bekommen davon, und Blutbäche verloren sich in seinem Fell. Er war zu zäh, sie mußten ihm erst eine Extrasalve bewilligen, ehe auch er in die Knie ging.»

Leo and Budd, too, thought it all very funny, and there was no end to Vinka's deceptively innocent questions; she was in full flight and didn't even notice that I was nudging her.

I had got drunk more quickly than I had intended; I was furious with her; she had no right to make fun of Wittigkeit, no one had a right to do that. Wittigkeit had been shepherd to the estate for twenty years and towards the end his herd had numbered over eight hundred head. He could castrate rams and help the ewes when they were lambing. He could light a fire from wet wood, and from the flight of the snipe he could tell what the coming summer was going to be like. He could put the broken leg of a sheep into splints so that it would grow together again in two weeks, and with his knife he knew how to make whistles that could decoy the oriole and the hoopoe. No one had a right to make fun of him; neither here nor anywhere else.

But they were all doing it; the whole club was laughing at him. He didn't notice it. He sat there wearing the jacket covered with plaster dust, and a grubby scarf of artificial silk, with his cap over his knee and glass in hand – he had put his other hand on Vinka's shoulder – and talked and talked, and drank and talked.

'And in the end,' he said, 'they killed off the whole herd; in order to prevent them falling into the hands of the Russians, they said. They set up machine-guns round about the pen and fired into it. At first only a few fell, but more and more did when they had been thinned out a bit. The front legs always went first, the back legs held firm.

'Then they laid their heads on one side, and then the rump, too, gave way. And finally, there was only the old bell-wether left. He had been hit any number of

Wittigkeit sah durch Vinka hindurch. Die räusperte sich, ihre Unterlippe zitterte.

«Warum tanzt eigentlich keiner mit mir?» fragte sie plötzlich gereizt.

«Lieber Himmel, ja–!» Budd stand auf. «Komm, du Blume von Soho.»

«Tja, denn», [11] sagte Leo unsicher und schenkte Wittigkeit ein.

Wittigkeit nahm das Glas und stand auf. Sein Halstuch war ihm aus der Joppe gerutscht, es hing ihm lang und dünn, fast wie ein Strick, vor dem Bauch; er schwankte und sah sich im Raum um. «Nichts–» sagte er auf einmal und fegte langsam die Gläser und die Flaschen vom Tisch: «nichts. Außer dir,» sagte er und ging mit seinem Glas schwankend zu Vistral hinüber.

Gleich brach die Kapelle mittendrin ab, nur der Schlagzeuger ließ den Drahtbesen noch sanft auf der Trommel vibrieren; keiner sprach; sie erhoben sich schweigend von den Tischen und reckten die Hälse; und auch die Tanzpaare ließen sich jetzt los und sahen zu Wittigkeit rüber. Denn jeder wußte, daß Vistral am Abend gegen Tschapczik verloren hatte, und jeder wußte aber auch, daß Vistral alles, selbst eine Niederlage, ertrug, nur eins nicht: nach einer Niederlage angesprochen zu werden.

Einmal hatten die Hunde nicht aufgepaßt, und ein Lamm war verlorengegangen. Wittigkeit suchte es die ganze Nacht. Am Morgen fand er es, es war in eine Grube gestürzt und hatte sich beide Vorderbeine gebrochen. Er schiente sie ihm und trug das Tier vier Wochen mit sich herum und nährte es mit der Flasche. Eines Tages aber stellte er es wieder auf die Erde, und da stand es und zitterte, und zwei Tage später nahm er ihm die Schienen ab und stützte es unter dem Bauch und machte die ersten Gehversuche mit ihm und nicht lange, und es lief wieder wie

times, and his eyes were full of red, and rivers of blood lost themselves in his hide. He was too tough; they had to give him an extra burst all to himself before he too sank to his knees.'

Wittigkeit was looking right through Vinka. She cleared her throat, and her lower lip was trembling.

'Why hasn't anyone asked me to dance?' she asked, suddenly irritable.

'But of course, of course, how could we forget!' Budd got up. 'Come dance with me, fair flower of Soho.'

'Well, well, then; let's have another drink,' said Leo uncertainly, and filled Wittigkeit's glass.

Wittigkeit took the glass and stood up. His scarf had slipped out of his jacket and dangled long and thin down his front, almost like a rope; he swayed and looked round the room. 'Nothing –' he said suddenly, and slowly swept the glasses and the bottles off the table. 'Nothing. Except you,' he said, and went swaying, glass in hand, over to Vistral.

The band broke off immediately at this, except for the drummer who continued to play a soft roll with his brush. No one spoke; they got up in silence from the tables and stretched their necks; the dancing couples parted and looked over at Wittigkeit. For everyone knew that Vistral had lost his fight with Tschapczik that evening, and everyone knew as well that Vistral could take anything, even a defeat, but that there was one thing he could not stand – being spoken to after he had lost.

One time the dogs had not been watchful enough and a lamb had been lost. Wittigkeit looked for it the whole night. He found it in the morning; it had fallen into a ditch and broken both front legs. He put them into splints, and carried the animal around with him for four

sonst, und seine Beine waren geheilt.

Wittigkeit stand jetzt unmittelbar vor Vistral. Der hatte seinen gelockten Bärenkopf angehoben und sah blinzelnd zu ihm auf.

«Du erinnerst mich an unsern Inspektor,» sagte Wittigkeit zu ihm. «Hat eine Menge von Schafen verstanden und ist auch sonst sehr vernünftig gewesen. Stoß mit mir an.»[12]

Vistral stand gar nicht erst auf, er schlug aus dem Sitz. Wittigkeit fiel hintenüber und riß zwei Tische mit um. Ich sprang auf und half ihm, sich aus den Tischtüchern zu wühlen.

Als wir uns aufrichteten, stand ein Kreis von Lachern um uns herum. Wittigkeit schien wieder nüchtern geworden zu sein. Er blutete am Kinn; auch seine Hand war blutig, er hielt noch den Stiel des abgebrochenen Weinglases fest, mit der anderen tastete er über sein Kinn. Ausgerechnet da fiel mir ein, daß Wittigkeit diese Erniedrigung nie widerfahren wäre, hätte ich ihn an der Baustelle nicht angesprochen. Aber wer kann das: ein Stück unversehrter Vergangenheit sehen und dran vorbeigehen. Ich hatte plötzlich den Wunsch, bis zur Besinnungslosigkeit verhauen zu werden. Ich sah mich gar nicht erst um, ich schlug blindlings in so ein bleiches, großrandig bebrilltes Jünglingsgesicht rein, und dann in ein zweites und drittes, und Budd bekam auch noch was ab. Dann erst kriegten sie mich. Ich bekam eine Kinnhakenserie, sie schlugen mich mit dem Kopf auf den Tisch, ich fiel hin, sie traten nach mir, sie packten mich; und dann rissen sie die Tür auf und warfen mich raus.

weeks, feeding it from a bottle. One day he set it on the ground again and it stood there trembling; two days later he took the splints off, supported it while it made its first attempts at walking, and it wasn't long before it could run as well as ever, its legs healed.

Wittigkeit was now standing right in front of Vistral. Vistral had lifted his curly, bear-like head and was blinking up at him.

'You remind me of our land-agent,' Wittigkeit said to him. 'Knew a lot about sheep, he did, and he was a very sensible chap all round. Here's to you.'

Vistral struck him without even waiting to get up. Wittigkeit fell over backwards, knocking down a couple of tables. I jumped up and helped him to disentangle himself from the table-cloths.

When we stood up there was a circle of laughing faces around us. Wittigkeit seemed to have sobered up again. His chin was bleeding and there was blood on his hand; he was still gripping the stem of the smashed wine-glass and with his free hand he was feeling his chin. Just at that very moment, of course, it had to occur to me that Wittigkeit would never have been humiliated in this way if I hadn't spoken to him at the building-site. But who can see something from the past that has survived intact and pass it by? I suddenly felt a desire to be beaten until I lost consciousness. I lashed out into one of these pale faces behind the thick-rimmed spectacles, and then into a second and a third, and Budd too came in for something. Not until then did they get me. I took a few hooks to the chin and they beat my head on the table. I fell down; they kicked out at me; they seized hold of me; and then they tore open the door and threw me out.

WHEN POTEMKIN'S COACH
WENT BY

REINHARD LETTAU

Translated by Marie Surridge

11. April 1787

Gestern abend kam Befehl aus Sewastopol, wir sollten hierbleiben und abwarten, was mit uns geschehen werde. Auch nach Durchfahrt der Kutsche, so scheint es, will man uns noch hierbehalten. Das leuchtet ein, haben wir uns doch[1] so weit von unseren heimatlichen Dörfern entfernt, daß wir, noch ehe wir den Bau dieses Dorfes begannen, uns ohnehin regelrechte Schlafstätten verschaffen mußten. Zunächst bauten wir also einfache Katen, wobei wir teilweise das von der Regierung zum Bau des angeblichen Dorfes vorgesehene Material benutzten. Diesen bescheidenen Unterkünften, die wir zu beiden Seiten des Weges anlegten, bauten wir dann die Fassaden des bestellten Dorfes vor. Zum Beispiel befindet sich mein Quartier direkt hinter jener recht hohen Holzwand, die von der Straße her wie ein Rathaus aussieht. Man öffnet die zu ebener Erde befindliche Tür des Rathauses und stößt direkt auf meine Hütte.[2] Hier liege ich Tag und Nacht und höre mir die Rapporte der Vormänner an. Meist handelt es sich ja nur um Maler. «Väterchen Aufseher,»[3] sagen sie, «was soll nun geschehen?» und ich diene ihnen mit Rat.

Die Dachdecker sind natürlich nur Maler, die Glaser sind Maler, die die Fenster mit geschickten Pinseln einpassen. Auch die Kaminbauer[4] sind Maler und die Steinmetzen, und die einzigen Leute, die hier Wirkliches leisten, sind jene Kulissenarbeiter, die die Gerüste erstellten und übri-

WHEN POTEMKIN'S COACH
WENT BY

11 April 1787

We received orders yesterday from Sevastopol to wait here until we are told what is to become of us. They want to keep us here, it seems, even after the coach has passed through. That is understandable, since we have come so far from our home villages that, before we began work on this village, we were in any case obliged to provide ourselves with proper sleeping-quarters. First of all, therefore, we set up simple shacks, using some of the materials the authorities had allotted for the sham village. We laid out these modest dwellings on either side of the road, and then in front of them erected the façades of the village we were commanded to build. My quarters, for instance, are to be found directly behind the fairly high wooden wall which, seen from the street, passes for a town hall. You open the door on the ground floor of the town hall, and come straight up against my hut. Here I lie day and night, receiving the reports of the foremen. For the most part, in fact, they are only painters. 'Guv'nor' they say, 'what is to happen now?' and I offer them my advice.

Of course, the thatchers are only painters, as are the glaziers whose skilled brushes put in the windows. The bricklayers and stonemasons, too, are painters, and the only people who produce anything real here are the scene-setters who built the scaffolding, and who

gens auch beim Bau unserer Unterkünfte Hand anlegten. Seither hat man sie aber nicht mehr tätig gesehen. Man berichtet mir, daß sie hinter der Holzwand, die sich von der Straßenseite her als Schenke ausgibt, herumliegen und dauernd trinken. Einem von ihnen soll es neulich gefallen haben, eines der weniger gut gelungenen Fenster im Orte einzuwerfen und durch ein wirkliches zu ersetzen. Wenn diese Übung um sich greift, so fürchte ich fast um das Gelingen meines Auftrags.

12. April 1787

Was ich mit dem letzten Satz meiner gestrigen Aufzeichnung meinte, ist am besten durch die Tatsache illustriert, daß in der Zwischenzeit mehr und mehr falsche Fensterfronten durch echte ersetzt worden sind. Einer der Glaser, ein gewisser Popow aus Nikolajew, wirklich ja ein Maler, beschwerte sich heute bei mir. «Unser ehrliches Werk,» rief er, «wird entstellt. Man hat kaum den Pinsel aus der Hand gelegt, da kommen schon Menschen und ersetzen unsere Gemälde durch wirkliche Fenster.»

Manchmal ergebe ich mich dem Eindruck, daß wir in Wirklichkeit zwei Dörfer bauen: ein falsches und ein richtiges, und zwar ohne das richtige zu wollen, indem dieses sich wie von selbst aus dem falschen erhebt, als liege eine Notwendigkeit vor.

13. April 1787

Heute wurde ich durch einen Angsttraum aus meinem Nachmittagsschläfchen gerüttelt. Mir träumte, die Kutsche komme endlich durchs Dorf, die Kaiserin befinde sich aber in einem tiefen Schläfchen, aus dem selbst der Fürst sie nicht zu wecken wage.[5] Nun sage ich mir, daß sie sich ja auch gerade in den Armen ihres Liebhabers, eben des Fürsten Potemkin,[6] befinden könne, während die Kutsche durch

incidentally also gave us some help with our huts. Since then, however, they have not been seen to work. I am told that they spend their time lounging and drinking behind the façade which from the street side purports to be an inn. They say it was one of them who recently thought fit to break in one of the less well executed windows in the village and put a real one in its place. If this practice once takes hold, I am almost fearful for the outcome of this commission.

12 April 1787

What I meant by the last sentence of yesterday's entry is best illustrated by the fact that in the meantime more and more false windows have been replaced by genuine ones. One of the glaziers, a certain Popov from Nikolayev, who is really of course a painter, came and complained to me today. 'Our honest work is being ruined,' he cried. 'We hardly have time to put down our paintbrushes before other men come and put real windows in place of our paintings.'

I find myself often under the impression that we are building two villages: one false and one real. Not that the real one is intended: it seems to grow out of the false one, as though by some sort of compulsion.

13 April 1787

I was shaken out of my midday nap today by a nightmarish dream. I dreamt that the coach was at last passing through the village, but the Empress had fallen into a deep sleep, from which even the prince did not dare to wake her. Now I keep thinking that as the coach is rushing through our street, she might just happen to be in the arms of her lover Prince Potemkin. Perhaps her eyes

unsere Straße rase. Und vielleicht wird sie nur einen
Augenaufschlag lang nach draußen blicken. Mir ist klar,
daß wir nur wegen der Möglichkeit dieses winzigen Aus-
blicks hier sind. Ich habe Pravdin gebeten, besonders die
Giebel unserer Siedlung hinsichtlich dieses möglichen Aus-
blicks noch einmal kritisch zu mustern.

Atemlos kam soeben Petrow gelaufen[7] und vertraute mir
an, daß aus dem von ihm jüngst gemalten Schornstein
wirklicher Rauch emporsteige. Da ich keine Zeit hatte, der
Sache nachzugehen, sandte ich ihn zurück und bat ihn, die
betreffende Fassade von hinten zu betrachten. Man habe sie
nach hinten zu zum Hause ergänzt, rief er mir zu, noch ehe
er in meine Hütte eintrat. Bei allen Heiligen! Es sollte
mich nicht wundern, wenn morgen früh die Kirchen-
glocken zur Messe riefen.

17. April 1787

Mein oben gemeldeter Traum zeigt einen wunderlichen
Wandel an, wenn man ihn mit den Angstvorstellungen
vergleicht, die ich hatte, als ich zu allererst von meinem
Auftrag hörte. Mein erster Gedanke war damals: «Was,
wenn Katharina nun auszusteigen begehrte? Was, wenn
man sie hinter leere Fassaden führen müßte statt in warme
Stübchen?»

Der Leutnant Chochotatskij, von Odessa in eine der
neuen Garnisonen auf der Krim verlegt, sprach gestern
oder vorgestern hier vor, gerade als ich mich zu einem
Nickerchen niederlassen wollte. «Wo,» fragte er, «wo
beabsichtigt Ihr, Väterchen, jenes falsche Dorf zu bauen?»
Obwohl ich doch weiß, daß er ein Spaßvogel ist, wäre ich
beinahe aufgesprungen und hinausgerannt. Seit Tagen
ängstigt mich nun die Vorstellung, der Fürst könne sich
die gleiche Frage stellen. Heute haben wirklich die Kirchen-
glocken geläutet und Petrow berichtet mir, daß nun Rauch

will glance out towards us for no more than a second. I realize that we are here because of the possibility that she may give us just such a tiny glance. I have asked Pravdin to look carefully once more at the roof-tops of our settlement with the possibility of this glance in mind.

Just then Petrov came panting in, to tell me that real smoke was rising from the chimneys he himself had so recently painted. Since I had no time to look into the matter, I sent him back with orders to look at the façade in question from behind. He shouted even before he was back in the hut that it had been built out at the back so as to make a real house. By all that's holy! I should not be surprised if the church bells rang for mass tomorrow morning.

17 April 1787

The dream I have been describing is in curious contrast to the anxious visions which came to me when I first heard of this project. My first thought then was: 'What if Catherine asked to be set down? What if we were obliged to take her behind hollow façades rather than into warm little rooms?'

Lieutenant Khokhotatsky, who has just been moved from Odessa to one of the new garrisons in the Crimea, called in yesterday or the day before, when I was about to lie down for a little nap. 'Well, little father,' he said, 'where are you thinking of building that sham village?' Although I know he is a joker, I almost jumped up and ran out of the room. For days I have been worried by the idea that the Prince might ask himself the same question. The church bells really did ring today, and Petrov tells me that smoke is now coming from all the chimneys,

aus allen Schornsteinen steige, daß man sich in unzähligen
Fenstern, hinter denen man Blümchen in echten Vasen
aufgestellt sehe, spiegeln könne. Die Schlosser, Glaser,
Dachdecker, Kaminbauer usw. sollen auch keine Farb-
flecken mehr an ihren Kitteln haben, und ganz in der Nähe
meiner Behausung, gewissermaßen Wand an Wand, höre
ich Menschen arbeiten. Es sollte mich nicht wundern, wenn
ich eines Tages entdeckte, daß meine Hütte ein Raum im
Rathaus ist.

19. April 1787

Diesen Gedanken konnte ich nicht mehr verdrängen,
seit ich Geräusche von oberhalb meiner Kate höre, so, als
liefe man dort herum. Die Versuchung, aufzustehen und
die Sache zu untersuchen, is groß. Es besteht ja die Gefahr,
daß der Fürst dieses Dorf für ein richtiges Dorf halten wird.
Und dann wird er mich fragen, wo ich das falsche, das von
ihm bestellte, denn gebaut habe? Wird er nicht mutmaßen,
ich hätte das Material, das mir von der Regierung anver-
traut worden ist, verkauft? Jedenfalls habe ich Anweisung
gegeben, in Eile den der Dorfstraße zugekehrten Häuser-
fronten den geradezu stümperhaften Anschein von Kulissen zu geben. Während ich dies schreibe, sind die Glaser
und Dachdecker, Kaminbauer und Schlosser emsig wie
Ameisen damit beschäftigt, das Werk ihrer Hände zu
überstreichen.

21. April 1787

An der glücklichen Vollendung dieser Arbeit bin ich
besonders interessiert, seit man mir gestern meine ein-
mütige Erwählung zum Dorfältesten mitgeteilt hat.[8] Meine
Bestallung lag nahe, denn das Rathaus ist nun fertiggestellt.
In Stundenfrist[9] wird man eine andere Tür in meine Hütte
brechen, die mich, wenn ich je aufstünde, auf den Korridor

that one can see one's face reflected in countless windows, and look through them at flowers arranged in real vases. It is said that the fitters, glaziers, thatchers, bricklayers, and so on now have no paint-splashes on their smocks, and I can hear men working just near my quarters, as though they were in the next room. It would not surprise me if one day I found that my hut is a room in the town hall.

19 April 1787

I have been hearing noises above my hut, as though people were running about, and I can no longer keep this idea at bay. The temptation to get up and look into the matter is great. There certainly is some danger that the prince will take this to be a real village. And then he will ask me where I have put the sham one he ordered me to build. He will surely think I have sold the materials entrusted to me by the authorities. At any rate, I have given instructions that the houses which face the street must quickly be given the candidly slipshod appearance of stage sets. As I write this, the glaziers, thatchers, bricklayers, and fitters are as busy as ants, painting over their own handiwork.

21 April 1787

I am particularly concerned that this work should be brought to a happy conclusion, since I was told yesterday that I had been unanimously elected village elder. My installation was soon to come, it seemed, for the town hall is ready. In an hour's time, they are going to knock another door through into my hut which, if I were to rise and go to it, would take me into the corridor

des Rathauses und in eine Flucht angenehmer Räume
führen würde, die man mir dort hergerichtet haben will.

Ich muß mich unterbrechen. Man meldet das Nahen der
kaiserlichen Kutsche.

29. April 1787

Der Lärm, der bei der Aufbrechung der Wand entstand,
war ganz schrecklich. Ich selbst war genötigt, aufzustehen
und in die entgegengesetzte Ecke des Zimmers zu fliehen.
Noch jetzt klingt es in meinen Ohren nach. Man teilte mir
mit, daß es oft Wochen dauert, ehe man solche Erlebnisse
überwindet. Absolute Ruhe und vor allem Schlaf, dieser
Heiler allen Übels, empfiehlt sich.

Mein Präfekt wurde vorstellig. Es sei neulich die erwartete Kutsche mit dem kaiserlichen Wappen am Verschlag
hier durchgefahren. Die Arbeit am Schulbau schreitet
voran.

of the town hall, and a suite of rooms which they insist on preparing for me there.

I must pause here. They say the imperial coach is coming.

29 April 1787

The noise they made knocking through the wall was terrible. I myself was forced to get up and run to the opposite corner of the room. The din is still ringing in my ears. They told me it often takes weeks to recover from such experiences. Absolute quiet and above all sleep, that healer of all ills, are recommended.

My officer appeared. He said that the long-awaited coach bearing the imperial arms passed through here not long ago. Work on the school-house is progressing.

THITHYPHUTH,
OR MY UNCLE'S WAITER
WOLFGANG BORCHERT

Translated by Paul Dinnage

SCHISCHYPHUSCH

ODER DER KELLNER MEINES ONKELS

DABEI war mein Onkel natürlich kein Gastwirt. Aber er kannte einen Kellner. Dieser Kellner verfolgte[1] meinen Onkel so intensiv mit seiner Treue und mit seiner Verehrung, daß wir immer sagten: Das ist sein Kellner. Oder: Ach so, sein Kellner.

Als sie sich kennenlernten, mein Onkel und der Kellner, war ich dabei. Ich war damals gerade so groß, daß ich die Nase auf den Tisch legen konnte. Das durfte ich aber nur, wenn sie sauber war. Und immer konnte sie natürlich nicht sauber sein. Meine Mutter war auch nicht viel älter. Etwas älter war sie wohl, aber wir waren beide noch so jung, daß wir uns ganz entsetzlich schämten, als der Onkel und der Kellner sich kennenlernten. Ja, meine Mutter und ich, wir waren dabei.

Mein Onkel natürlich auch, ebenso wie der Kellner, denn die beiden sollten sich ja kennenlernen und auf sie kam es an. Meine Mutter und ich waren nur als Statisten dabei und hinterher haben wir es bitter verwünscht, daß wir dabei waren, denn wir mußten uns wirklich sehr schämen, als die Bekanntschaft der beiden begann. Es kam dabei nämlich zu allerhand erschrecklichen Szenen mit Beschimpfung, Beschwerden, Gelächter und Geschrei. Und beinahe hätte es sogar eine Schlägerei gegeben. Daß mein Onkel einen Zungenfehler[2] hatte, wäre beinahe der Anlaß zu dieser Schlägerei geworden. Aber daß er einbeinig war, hat die Schlägerei dann schließlich doch verhindert.

THITHYPHUTH,
OR MY UNCLE'S WAITER

NOT, of course, that my uncle managed a pub. But he did know a waiter. This waiter dogged my uncle with such devotion and respect that we always said, 'That's his waiter', or, 'Ah, *his* waiter'.

I was present when my uncle and the waiter became acquainted. I was then just big enough to rest my nose on the table. This I was only allowed to do if it – my nose – was clean. And of course it was not always clean. My mother too was not much older. She was necessarily somewhat older, but we were both so young that we were quite horrified when my uncle and the waiter met. Yes, my mother and I were there.

And my uncle of course, likewise the waiter, for the pair were destined to meet, and so it came to pass. My mother and I were only there as extras and we afterwards bitterly rued our presence, for really we could only be very ashamed when the pair's acquaintance began. In point of fact it led to all sorts of frightful scenes, with insults, complaints, laughter, and shouting. And there was almost a free fight. That my uncle had a speech defect was very nearly the occasion of this brawl. That he had only one leg finally prevented it.

Wir saßen also, wir drei, mein Onkel, meine Mutter und ich, an einem sonnigen Sommertag nachmittags in einem großen prächtigen bunten Gartenlokal. Um uns herum saßen noch ungefähr zwei- bis dreihundert andere Leute, die auch alle schwitzten. Hunde saßen unter den schattigen Tischen und Bienen saßen auf den Kuchentellern. Oder kreisten um die Limonadengläser der Kinder. Es war so warm und so voll, daß die Kellner alle ganz beleidigte Gesichter hatten, als ob das alles nur stattfände aus Schikane. Endlich kam auch einer an unseren Tisch.

Mein Onkel hatte, wie ich schon sagte, einen Zungenfehler. Nicht bedeutend, aber immerhin deutlich genug. Er konnte kein s sprechen. Auch kein z oder tz. Er brachte das einfach nicht fertig. Immer wenn in einem Wort so ein harter s-Laut auftauchte, dann machte er ein weiches feuchtwässeriges sch daraus. Und dabei schob er die Lippen weit vor, daß sein Mund entfernte Ähnlichkeit mit einem Hühnerpopo bekam.

Der Kellner stand also an unserem Tisch und wedelte mit seinem Taschentuch die Kuchenkrümel unserer Vorgänger von der Decke. (Erst viele Jahre später erfuhr ich, daß es nicht sein Taschentuch, sondern eine Art Serviette gewesen sein muß.) Er wedelte also damit und fragte kurzatmig und nervös:

«Bitte schehr? Schie wünschen?»

Mein Onkel, der keine alkoholarmen Getränke schätzte, sagte gewohnheitsmäßig:

«Alscho: Schwei Aschbach[3] und für den Jungen Schelter oder Brausche. Oder wasch haben Schie schonscht?»

Der Kellner war sehr blaß. Und dabei war es Hochsommer und er war doch Kellner in einem Gartenlokal. Aber vielleicht war er überarbeitet. Und plötzlich merkte ich, daß mein Onkel unter seiner blanken braunen Haut

So we three, my uncle, my mother, and myself, sat one sunny summer afternoon in a large, resplendent, gay beer-garden. Around us sat about two or three hundred other people, all perspiring. Dogs lay in the shade of the tables and bees settled on the plates of cakes. Or circled round the children's lemonade glasses. It was so hot and full that the waiters all wore injured looks, as though it were all a conspiracy. One of them at last came over to our table.

Now, as I was saying, my uncle had a speech defect. Not considerable, but nevertheless distinct enough. He couldn't pronounce an 's'. Nor a 'z' or 'tz'. He simply couldn't do it. When a hard 's' sound came up in a word, he came out with a weak, damp, watery 'th'. And in so doing he pursed his lips out so that his mouth bore a faint resemblance to a hen's backside.

Well, the waiter stood at our table, and flicked the cake-crumbs of our predecessors from the cloth with his handkerchief. (It was many years later that I learned that this must have been not his handkerchief but a kind of napkin.) So he flicked about with it and asked, short-breathed and nervous:

'Yeth pleath? Would you like thomething?'

My uncle, who had no love for non-alcoholic drinks, replied in his habitual way:

'Let'th thee. Two brandieth. And for the child a fithy drink or lemonade-thoda. Or what elthe have you?'

The waiter was very pale. And yet it was midsummer, and he was a waiter in a beer-garden. But perhaps he was overworked. And I suddenly noticed that under his clear brown skin my uncle had also turned pale. Ac-

auch blaß wurde. Nämlich als der Kellner die Bestellung
der Sicherheit wegen wiederholte:

«Schehr wohl. Schwei Aschbach. Eine Brausche. Bitte
schehr.»

Mein Onkel sah meine Mutter mit hochgezogenen
Brauen an, als ob er etwas Dringendes von ihr wollte. Aber
er wollte sich nur vergewissern, ob er noch auf dieser Welt
sei. Dann sagte er mit einer Stimme, die an fernen Ge-
schützdonner erinnerte:

«Schagen Schie mal, schind schie wahnschinnig? Schie?
Schie machen schich über mein Lischpeln luschtig? Wasch?»

Der Kellner stand da und dann fing es an, an ihm zu
zittern. Seine Hände zitterten. Seine Augendeckel. Seine
Knie. Vor allem aber zitterte seine Stimme. Sie zitterte vor
Schmerz und Wut und Fassungslosigkeit, als er sich jetzt
Mühe gab, auch etwas geschützdonnerähnlich zu antworten:

«Esch ischt schamlosch von Schie, schich über mich schu
amüschieren, taktlosch ischt dasch, bitte schehr.»

Nun zitterte alles an ihm. Seine Jackenzipfel. Seine
pomadenverklebten Haarsträhnen. Seine Nasenflügel und
seine sparsame Unterlippe.

An meinem Onkel zitterte nichts. Ich sah ihn ganz genau
an: Absolut nichts. Ich bewunderte meinen Onkel. Aber
als der Kellner ihn schamlos nannte, da stand mein Onkel
doch wenigstens auf. Das heißt, er stand eigentlich gar
nicht auf. Das wäre ihm mit seinem einen Bein viel zu
umständlich und beschwerlich gewesen. Er blieb sitzen und
stand dabei doch auf. Innerlich stand er auf. Und das
genügte auch vollkommen. Der Kellner fühlte dieses
innerliche Aufstehen meines Onkels wie einen Angriff, und
er wich zwei kurze zittrige unsichere Schritte zurück.
Feindselig standen sie sich gegenüber. Obgleich mein
Onkel saß. Wenn er wirklich aufgestanden wäre, hätte sich
sehr wahrscheinlich der Kellner hingesetzt. Mein Onkel

tually, this was when the waiter repeated the order to confirm it:

'Very good. Two brandieth. A thoda. Thank you.'

My uncle looked at my mother with raised eyebrows, as if he expected something cogent from her. But he only wanted to reassure himself that he was still in this world. Then, in a voice reminiscent of the distant thunder of guns, he said:

'Jutht tell me, are you crathy? You? You're making fun of my lithp, eh?'

The waiter stood there, and then he began to tremble. His hands trembled. His eyelids. His knees. But above all his voice trembled. It trembled in pain and anger and incomprehension as he endeavoured to reply somewhat in the thunder-of-guns manner:

'It'th thcandalouth of you to amuthe yourthelf at my expenthe, it'th dithrethpectful, if you pleath.'

Now he trembled all over. The tails of his jacket. His smarmed-down strands of hair. His nostrils and his scant lower lip.

No part of my uncle shook. I looked at him scrupulously; absolutely no part. I admired my uncle. But when the waiter called him scandalous, then at least my uncle stood up. That is to say, he by no means stood up properly speaking. With his one leg, that would have been much too formal and difficult. He remained seated and nevertheless stood up. He stood up within himself. Which, too, was perfectly adequate. The waiter felt this inner rising of my uncle's like an offensive, and he fell back a couple of short, shaky, uncertain steps. Hostile, they stood facing one another. Although my uncle sat. If he really had stood up, the waiter would probably have sat down. And my uncle could afford

konnte es sich auch leisten, sitzen zu bleiben, denn er war
noch im Sitzen ebenso groß wie der Kellner, und ihre
Köpfe waren auf gleicher Höhe.

So standen sie nun und sahen sich an. Beide mit einer zu
kurzen Zunge, beide mit demselben Fehler. Aber jeder mit
einem völlig anderen Schicksal.

Klein, verbittert, verarbeitet, zerfahren, fahrig, farblos,
verängstigt, unterdrückt: der Kellner. Der kleine
Kellner. Ein richtiger Kellner: Verdrossen, stereotyp
höflich, geruchlos, ohne Gesicht, numeriert, verwaschen
und trotzdem leicht schmuddelig. Ein kleiner Kellner.
Zigarettenfingrig, servil, steril, glatt, gut gekämmt,
blaurasiert, gelbgeärgert,[4] mit leerer Hose hinten und
dicken Taschen an der Seite, schiefen Absätzen und
chronisch verschwitztem Kragen – der kleine Kellner.

Und mein Onkel? Ach, mein Onkel! Breit, braun,
brummend, baßkehlig, laut, lachend, lebendig, reich,
riesig, ruhig, sicher, satt, saftig – mein Onkel!

Der kleine Kellner und mein großer Onkel. Verschieden
wie ein Karrengaul vom Zeppelin. Aber beide kurzzungig.
Beide mit demselben Fehler. Beide mit einem feuchten
wässerigen weichen sch. Aber der Kellner ausgestoßen,
getreten von seinem Zungenschicksal, bockig, eingeschüchtert, enttäuscht, einsam, bissig.

Und klein, ganz klein geworden. Tausendmal am Tag
verspottet, an jedem Tisch belächelt, belacht, bemitleidet,
begrinst, beschrien. Tausendmal an jedem Tag im Gartenlokal an jedem Tisch einen Zentimeter in sich hineinge-
krochen, geduckt, geschrumpft. Tausendmal am Tag bei
jeder Bestellung an jedem Tisch, bei jedem «bitte schehr»
kleiner, immer kleiner geworden. Die Zunge, gigantischer
unförmiger Fleischlappen, die viel zu kurze Zunge,
formlose zyklopische Fleischmasse, plumper unfähiger

to remain seated, for seated he was as large as the waiter, and their heads were on the same level.

So now they stood and looked at each other. Both with a too-short tongue, both with the same deficiency. But each with a completely different destiny.

Little, embittered, toil-worn, preoccupied, fidgety, pale, cowed, crushed: the waiter. The little waiter. A genuine waiter: sullen, conventionally polite, odourless, faceless, numbered, scrubbed yet even so slightly scruffy. A little waiter. Nicotine-fingered, servile, sterile, bland, well-combed, blue-shaven, fed up to the teeth, nothing to fill his trousers with behind and bulging pockets either side, down-at-heel and with a perpetually sweat-stained collar – the little waiter.

And my uncle? Oh, my uncle! Broad, brown, bumbling, bass-voiced, loud, laughing, living, copious, colossal, calm, secure, satisfied, salacious – my uncle!

The little waiter and my large uncle. Different as a dray-horse and a dirigible. But both short-tongued. Both with the same defect. Both with a damp, watery, weak 'th'. But the waiter a pariah, down-trodden by his fatal tongue, mutinous, intimidated, disappointed, lonely, testy.

And become quite, quite small. Ridiculed a thousand times a day, smiled at, laughed at, pitied, smirked at, and bawled at from every table. A thousand times every day at every table in the beer-garden retracting a centimetre within himself, humbled and crumpled. A thousand times every day at every order at every table, at every 'pleath', becoming ever smaller and smaller. The tongue, that giant, amorphous lobe of flesh, the much-too-short tongue, that shapeless cyclopean lump of flesh,

roter Muskelklumpen, diese Zunge hatte ihn zum Pygmäen erdrückt: kleiner, kleiner Kellner!

Und mein Onkel! Mit einer zu kurzen Zunge, aber: als hätte er sie nicht. Mein Onkel, selbst am lautesten lachend, wenn über ihn gelacht wurde. Mein Onkel, einbeinig, kolossal, slickzungig. Aber Apoll in jedem Zentimeter Körper und jedem Seelenatom. Autofahrer, Frauenfahrer, Herrenfahrer, Rennfahrer. Mein Onkel, Säufer, Sänger, Gewaltmensch, Witzereißer, Zotenflüsterer, Verführer, kurzzungiger sprühender sprudelnder spuckender Anbeter von Frauen und Kognak. Mein Onkel, saufender Sieger, prothesenknarrend, breitgrinsend, mit viel zu kurzer Zunge, aber: als hätte er sie nicht!

So standen sie sich gegenüber. Mordbereit, todwund der eine, lachfertig, randvoll mit Gelächtereruptionen der andere. Ringsherum sechs- bis siebenhundert Augen und Ohren, Spazierläufer, Kaffeetrinker, Kuchenschleckerer, die den Auftritt mehr genossen als Bier und Brause und Bienenstich.[5] Ach, und mittendrin meine Mutter und ich. Rotköpfig, schamhaft, tief in die Wäsche verkrochen. Und unsere Leiden waren erst am Anfang.

«Schuchen Schie schofort den Wirt, Schie aggreschiver Schpatz, Schie. Ich will Schie lehren, Gäschte schu inschultieren.»

Mein Onkel sprach jetzt absichtlich so laut, daß den sechs- bis siebenhundert Ohren kein Wort entging. Der Asbach regte ihn in angenehmer Weise an. Er grinste vor Wonne über sein großes gutmütiges breites braunes Gesicht. Helle salzige Perlen kamen aus der Stirn und trudelten abwärts über die massiven Backenknochen. Aber der Kellner hielt alles an ihm für Bosheit, für Gemeinheit, für Beleidigung und Provokation. Er stand mit faltigen hohlen leise wehenden Wangen da und rührte sich nicht von der Stelle.

that unwieldy, incompetent, red conglomeration of muscle, that tongue had reduced him to a pygmy: little, little waiter!

And my uncle! But with a too-short tongue; as if he had none. My uncle, laughing loudest himself when he was laughed at. My uncle, one-legged, gigantic, lisp-tongued. But an Apollo in every inch of his body and every atom of his soul. Car driver, woman driver, man driver, racing driver. My uncle, boozer, singer, strong-arm man, joke merchant, smut-mutterer, seducer, short-tongued spraying sputtering spitting devotee of women and brandy. My uncle, carousing conqueror, artificial limb creaking, broad-grinning, with his much-too-short tongue, though; as if he had none.

So they stood facing one another. Murderous and mortally wounded the one, jovial and brimming with explosive laughter the other. All around, six to seven hundred eyes and ears, saunterers, coffee-drinkers, cake-guzzlers, who enjoyed the scene more than beer, fizz, and honey-cakes. Oh, and my mother and I in the middle of it all. Red to the roots, ashamed, cringing into our clothes. And this was only the beginning of our sorrows.

'Pleath find the landlord at onthe, you aggrethive thparrow, you. I'll teatth you to inthult cuthtomerth.'

My uncle now spoke so purposefully loud that the six to seven hundred ears missed not a word. The brandy pleasantly stimulated him. He grinned with delight all over his great, genial, broad, brown face. Shining salty pearls broke out on his brow and rolled down over the massive cheekbones. But the waiter took this in him for malevolence, mean trickery, insult, and provocation. He stood there with puckered, hollow, slightly quivering cheeks and did not move from the spot.

«Haben Schie Schand in den Gehörgängen? Schuchen Schie den Beschitscher, Schie beschoffener Schpaschvogel. Losch, oder haben Schie die Hosche voll, Schie mischgeschtalteter Schwerg?»

Da faßte der kleine Pygmäe, der kleine slickzungige Kellner, sich ein großmütiges, gewaltiges, für uns alle und für ihn selbst überraschendes Herz. Er trat ganz nah an unsern Tisch, wedelte mit seinem Taschentuch über unsere Teller und knickte zu einer korrekten Kellnerverbeugung zusammen. Mit einer kleinen männlichen und entschlossen leisen Stimme, mit überwältigender zitternder Höflichkeit sagte er: «Bitte schehr!» und setzte sich klein, kühn und kaltblütig auf den vierten freien Stuhl an unserem Tisch. Kaltblütig natürlich nur markiert. Denn in seinem tapferen kleinen Kellnerherzen flackerte die empörte Flamme der verachteten gescheuchten mißgestalteten Kreatur. Er hatte auch nicht den Mut, meinen Onkel anzusehen. Er setzte sich nur so klein und sachlich hin, und ich glaube, daß höchstens ein Achtel seines Gesäßes den Stuhl berührte. (Wenn er überhaupt mehr als ein Achtel besaß – vor lauter Bescheidenheit.) Er saß, sah vor sich hin auf die kaffeeübertropfte grauweiße Decke, zog seine dicke Brieftasche hervor und legte sie immerhin einigermaßen männlich auf den Tisch. Eine halbe Sekunde riskierte er einen kurzen Aufblick, ob er wohl zu weit gegangen sei mit dem Aufbumsen der Tasche, dann, als er sah, daß der Berg, mein Onkel nämlich, in seiner Trägheit verharrte, öffnete er die Tasche und nahm ein Stück pappartiges zusammengeknifftes Papier heraus, dessen Falten das typische Gelb eines oftbenutzten Stück Papiers aufwiesen. Er klappte es wichtig auseinander, verkniff sich jeden Ausdruck von Beleidigtsein oder Rechthaberei und legte sachlich seinen kurzen abgenutzten Finger auf eine bestimmte Stelle des Stück

'Have you got thand in your ear-holth? Call the owner, you thothled thimpleton. Off with you, or have you thit yourthelf, you miththapen thprite?'

Then the little pygmy, the little lisp-tongued waiter, took courage – a magnanimous, huge courage, surprising for us all and for himself. He stepped up quite close to our table, flicked over our plates with his handkerchief and bowed a correct waiter's bow. With a tiny, masculine, decisive, and low voice, with an overwhelming, trembling politeness, he said: 'If you pleath!' and sat, brief, bold, nonchalant, on the free, fourth chair at our table. Of course only simulated nonchalance. For in his brave little waiter's heart there flared the rebellious flame of a creature despised, frightened, misshapen. And yet he had not the courage to look at my uncle. He merely sat down, so small and pertinent, and I think that at the most an eighth of his bottom was in contact with the chair. (If he had more than an eighth at all – out of sheer modesty.) He sat, looked in front of him at the grey-white coffee-spotted table-cloth, drew out his bulky wallet and laid it on the table, still something of a man. He risked a brief look up for half a second, although he had already gone too far by plumping down his wallet, then, when he saw that the mountain, i.e. my uncle, persisted in its immovableness, he opened the wallet and drew out a piece of clipped-up cardboard-like paper, whose folds showed the characteristic yellow of a well-worn piece of paper. He snapped it open with much ado, dispensed with any expression of being the injured party or of seeking redress, and pointedly laid his stubby, worn finger on a particular place of the piece of paper. He added softly, a mite more hoarse and with long pauses for breath:

Papiers. Dazu sagte er leise, eine Spur heiser und mit großen Atempausen:

«Bitte schehr. Wenn Schie schehen wollen. Schtellen Schie höflichscht schelbscht fescht. Mein Pasch. In Parisch geweschen. Barschelona. Oschnabrück, bitte schehr. Allesch ausch meinem Pasch schu erschehen. Und hier: Beschondere Kennscheichen: Narbe am linken Knie. (Vom Fußballspiel.) Und hier, und hier? Wasch ischt hier? Hier, bitte schehr: Schprachfehler scheit Geburt. Bitte schehr. Wie Schie schelbscht schehen!»

Das Leben war zu rabenmütterlich[6] mit ihm umgegangen, als daß er jetzt den Mut gehabt hätte, seinen Triumph auszukosten und meinen Onkel herausfordernd anzusehen. Nein, er sah still und klein vor sich auf seinen vorgestreckten Finger und den bewiesenen Geburtsfehler und wartete geduldig auf den Baß meines Onkels.

Es dauerte nicht lange, bis der kam. Und als er dann kam, war es so unerwartet, was er sagte, daß ich vor Schreck einen Schluckauf bekam. Mein Onkel ergriff plötzlich mit seinen klobigen viereckigen Tatmenschenhänden die kleinen flatterigen Pfoten des Kellners und sagte mit der vitalen wütend-kräftigen Gutmütigkeit und der tierhaft warmen Weichheit, die als primärer Wesenszug aller Riesen gilt: «Armesch kleinesch Luder! Schind schie schon scheit deiner Geburt hinter dir her und hetschen?»

Der Kellner schluckte. Dann nickte er. Nickte sechs-, siebenmal. Erlöst. Befriedigt. Stolz. Geborgen. Sprechen konnte er nicht. Er begriff nichts. Verstand und Sprache waren erstickt von zwei dicken Tränen. Sehen konnte er auch nicht, denn die zwei dicken Tränen schoben sich vor seine Pupillen wie zwei undurchsichtige allesversöhnende Vorhänge. Er begriff nichts. Aber sein Herz empfing diese Welle des Mitgefühls wie eine Wüste, die tausend Jahre auf einen Ozean gewartet hatte. Bis an sein Lebensende

'Pleath. If you would pleath look. Motht courteouth
if you would make thertain for yourthelf. My pathport.
Been in Parith. Barthelona. Othnabrück, pleath. Thee
it all in my pathport. And here – Thpethial Peculiaritieth
– thcar on left knee (from playing thoccer). And here,
here? What'th thith here? Here, pleath: Thpeech defect
thinthe birth. If you pleath. Ath you can thee for yourthelf!'

Life had treated him too uncharitably for him now to
have the courage to enjoy his triumph to the full and
challenge my uncle with a look. No, still and small, he
looked at his outstretched finger and the demonstrable
born defect and waited patiently for my uncle's bass.

It was not long in coming. And when it came, what
he said was so unexpected that I hiccupped with fright.
My uncle, with his clumsy, four-square, man-of-action
hands, suddenly seized the tiny fluttering paws of the
waiter and said, with the vital, power-and-fury bon-
homie and warm animal tenderness which is the primary
characteristic of all giants: 'Poor little beatht! Have they
been baiting you ever thinth birth?'

The waiter gulped. Then he nodded. Nodded six,
seven times. Saved. Satisfied. Proud. Out of danger. He
could not speak. He comprehended nothing. Understanding and speech were choked by two ample tears.
Nor could he see, for the two fat tears rose before his
pupils like two opaque, all-appeasing curtains. He comprehended nothing. But his heart received this wave of
sympathy like a desert that had waited a thousand years
for an ocean. He could have let himself be flooded over
like this to the end of his life; until death he could have

hätte er sich so überschwemmen lassen können! Bis an seinen Tod hätte er seine kleinen Hände in der Pranken meines Onkels verstecken mögen! Bis in die Ewigkeit hätte er das hören können, dieses: Armesch, kleinesch Luder!

Aber meinem Onkel dauerte das alles schon zu lange. Er war Autofahrer. Auch wenn er im Lokal saß. Er ließ seine Stimme wie eine Artilleriesalve über das Gartenlokal hinwegdröhnen und donnerte irgendeinen erschrockenen Kellner an:

«Schie, Herr Ober! Acht Aschbach! Aber losch, schag ich Ihnen? Wasch? Nicht Ihr Revier?[7] Bringen Schie schofort acht Aschbach oder tun Schie dasch nicht, wasch?»

Der fremde Kellner sah eingeschüchtert und verblüfft auf meinen Onkel. Dann auf seinen Kollegen. Er hätte ihm gern von den Augen abgesehen (durch ein Zwinkern oder so), was das alles zu bedeuten hätte. Aber der kleine Kellner konnte seinen Kollegen kaum erkennen, so weit weg war er von allem, was Kellner, Kuchenteller, Kaffeetasse und Kollege hieß, weit weit weg davon.

Dann standen acht Asbach auf dem Tisch. Vier Gläser davon mußte der fremde Kellner gleich wieder mitnehmen, sie waren leer, ehe er einmal geatmet hatte. «Laschen Schie dasch da nochmal vollaufen!» befahl mein Onkel und wühlte in den Innentaschen seiner Jacke. Dann pfiff er eine Parabel[8] durch die Luft und legte nun seinerseits seine dicke Brieftasche neben die seines neuen Freundes. Er fummelte endlich eine zerknickte Karte heraus und legte seinen Mittelfinger, der die Maße eines Kinderarms hatte, auf einen bestimmten Teil der Karte.

«Schiehscht du, dummesch Häschchen, hier schtehtsch: Beinamputiert und Unterkieferschusch. Kriegschverletschung.» Und während er das sagte, zeigte er mit der anderen Hand auf eine Narbe, die sich unterm Kinn versteckt hielt.

hidden his tiny hands in my uncle's clutches. Unto eternity he could have listened to this: 'Poor little beatht!'

But all this was going on too long for my uncle. He drove a car. Even when sitting in a pub. He let his voice boom out like a salvo of artillery over the beer-garden and thundered at some terrified waiter:

'You there, waiter! Eight brandieth! And tharp about it, I thay. What? Not your table? Eight brandieth at onthe, or do you refuthe, eh?'

The unknown waiter looked at my uncle, browbeaten and flabbergasted. Then at his colleague, who could readily have indicated by eye (by a wink or the like) what it was all about. But the little waiter could scarcely recognize this colleague, so far was he from all that bore the name of waiter, cake-plate, coffee-cup, and colleague, far, far from it.

Next, the eight brandies stood on the table. Immediately the strange waiter had to gather four glasses from it, which were empty before he had time to draw one breath. 'Fill 'em up onthe more!' ordered my uncle, and rummaged in the inside pocket of his jacket. Then he whistled a note that shot through the air and laid, for his part, his bulky wallet next to that of his new friend. He eventually fumbled out a dog-eared card and put his middle finger , which was as thick as a child's arm, on a specific part of it.

'You thee, you thtupid little donkey, here it ith: leg amputathion and lower maxillary wound. War wound.' And as he spoke, he pointed out with his other hand a scar which lay concealed under his chin.

«Die Öösch⁹ haben mir einfach ein Schtück von der Schungenschptische abgeschoschen. In Frankreich da malsch.»

Der Kellner nickte.

«Noch bösche?» fragte mein Onkel.

Der Kellner schüttelte schnell den Kopf hin und her, als wollte er etwas ganz Unmögliches abwehren.

«Ich dachte nur schuerscht, Schie wollten mich utschen.» Erschüttert über seinen Irrtum in der Menschenkenntnis wackelte er mit dem Kopf immer wieder von links nach rechts und wieder zurück.

Und nun schien es mit einmal, als ob er alle Tragik seines Schicksals damit abgeschüttelt hätte. Die beiden Tränen, die sich nun in den Hohlheiten seines Gesichtes verliefen, nahmen alle Qual seines bisherigen verspotteten Daseins mit. Sein neuer Lebensabschnitt, den er an der Riesentatze meines Onkels betrat, begann mit einem kleinen aufstoßenden Lacher, einem Gelächterchen, zage, scheu, aber von einem unverkennbaren Asbachgestank begleitet.

Und mein Onkel, dieser Onkel, der sich auf einem Bein, mit zerschossener Zunge und einem bärigen baßstimmigen Humor durch das Leben lachte, dieser mein Onkel war nun so unglaublich selig, daß er endlich endlich lachen konnte. Er war schon bronzefarben angelaufen, daß ich fürchtete, er müsse jede Minute platzen. Und sein Lachen lachte los, unbändig, explodierte, polterte, juchte, gongte,¹⁰ gurgelte – lachte los, als ob er ein Riesensaurier wäre, dem diese Urweltlaute entrülpsten. Das erste kleine neu probierte Menschlachen des Kellners, des neuen kleinen Kellnermenschen, war dagegen wie das schüttere Gehüstel eines erkälteten Ziegenbabys. Ich griff angstvoll nach der Hand meiner Mutter. Nicht daß ich Angst vor meinem Onkel gehabt hätte, aber ich hatte doch eine tiefe tierische Angstwitterung vor den acht Asbachs, die in meinem Onkel

'The bathtardth thimply thot a pieth off the tip of my tongue. In Franthe, it wath.'

The waiter nodded.

'Thtill upthet?' my uncle asked.

The waiter shook his head rapidly to and fro, as if he wanted to ward off something totally impossible.

'I only thought at firtht you wanted to teathe me.'

Shattered by his mistake in understanding human nature, he continued to wag his head from left to right and back again.

And now it seemed as if at once he had shaken off all the tragedy of his fate. The two tears, which now coursed down the hollows of his face, took with them all the torment of his hitherto derided existence. The new era in his life, on which he entered in my uncle's giant paw, began with a tiny, erupting laugh, a titter, timid, bashful, but accompanied by an unmistakable stench of brandy.

And my uncle, that uncle who laughed his way through life with one leg, a shot-up tongue, and a bear-like bass-voiced sense of humour, that uncle of mine was now so unbelievably happy that he finally, finally was able to laugh. By now he had blushed so bronze that I feared he might burst at any moment. And his laughter laughed out, tremendously; exploded, rumbled, huzza'd, resounded, gurgled – laughed as if he were a giant saurian from whom these primeval noises belched forth. The first little tentative man's laugh of the waiter, of the new little waiter-man, was, by contrast, like the thin snuffling of a cold-nipped kid goat. Anxiously I groped for my mother's hand. Not that I was frightened of my uncle, but I had a deep animal apprehension of the eight brandies that fomented within him. My mother's hand

brodelten. Die Hand meiner Mutter war eiskalt. Alles Blut
hatte ihren Körper verlassen, um den Kopf zu einem grellen
plakatenen Symbol der Schamhaftigkeit und des bürger-
lichen Anstandes zu machen. Keine Vierländer[11] Tomate
konnte ein röteres Rot ausstrahlen. Meine Mutter leuchtete.
Klatschmohn war blaß gegen sie. Ich rutschte tief von
meinem Stuhl unter den Tisch. Siebenhundert Augen
waren rund und riesig um uns herum. Oh, wie wir uns
schämten, meine Mutter und ich.

Der kleine Kellner, der unter dem heißen Alkoholatem
meines Onkels ein neuer Mensch geworden war, schien den
ersten Teil seines neuen Lebens gleich mit einer ganzen
Ziegenmeckerlachepoche beginnen zu wollen. Er mähte,
bähte, gnuckte[10] und gnickerte wie eine ganze Lämmer-
herde auf einmal. Und als die beiden Männer nun noch
vier zusätzliche Asbachs über ihre kurzen Zungen schüt-
teten, wurden aus den Lämmern, aus den rosigen dünn-
stimmigen zarten schüchternen kleinen Kellnerlämmern,
ganz gewaltige hölzern meckernde steinalte weißbärtige
blechscheppernde blödblökende Böcke.

Diese Verwandlung vom kleinen giftigen tauben ver-
kniffenen Bitterling zum andauernd, fortdauernd meckern-
den schenkelschlagenden geckernden[10] blechern blökenden
Ziegenbockmenschen war selbst meinem Onkel etwas
ungewöhnlich. Sein Lachen vergluckerte langsam wie ein
absaufender Felsen.[12] Er wischte sich mit dem Ärmel die
Tränen aus dem braunen breiten Gesicht und glotzte mit
asbachblanken sturerstaunten Augen auf den unter Lach-
stößen bebenden weißbejackten Kellnerzwerg. Um uns
herum feixten siebenhundert Gesichter. Siebenhundert
Augen glaubten, daß sie nicht richtig sahen. Siebenhundert
Zwerchfelle schmerzten. Die, die am weitesten ab saßen,
standen erregt auf, um sich ja nichts entgehen zu lassen. Es
war, also ob der Kellner sich vorgenommen hatte, fortan

was ice-cold. All the blood had drained up from her body to turn her head into a glaring advertising symbol of modesty and middle-class morality. No prize tomato could radiate a redder red. My mother shone. Poppies were pale beside her. I slid from my chair beneath the table. All around us, seven hundred pairs of eyes were round and huge. Oh, how ashamed we were, my mother and I!

The little waiter, who had become a new man under the hot alcoholic breath of my uncle, apparently wished to start the first part of his new life with a period of goat-ish bleating laughter. He baa'd and bleated, gaggled and guggled like a whole flock of lambs at once. And as the two men now knocked back four more additional brandies over their short tongues, out of the lambs, out of the pink thin-voiced soft shy little waiter-lambs there grew quite mighty rough-hewn bleating prim-ordial white-bearded metal-clattering rubbish-blattering rams.

This metamorphosis from the tiny venomous numb pinched misery to the persistent, prolonged bleating thigh-slapping racketing raucous rattling he-goat was strange even to my uncle. His laughter gurgled away like a stanched waterfall. He wiped the tears from his brown broad face with his sleeve and goggled with brandy-bright staring astonished eyes at the white-jacketed dwarf waiter rocking with quakes of laughter. Seven hundred faces were grinning all round us. Seven hundred pairs of eyes could not believe what they saw. Seven hundred midriffs were in agony. Those who sat farthest away stood up excitedly so that nothing escaped them. It was as if the waiter had resolved to pursue his life henceforth as a gigantic wicked bleating ram. And just now, after being submerged in his own laughter for

als ein riesenhafter boshaft bähender Bock sein Leben fortzusetzen. Neuerdings, nachdem er wie aufgezogen einige Minuten in seinem eigenen Gelächter untergegangen war, neuerdings bemühte er sich erfolgreich, zwischen den Lachsalven, die wie ein blechernes Maschinengewehrfeuer aus seinem runden Mund perlten, kurze schrille Schreie auszustoßen. Es gelang ihm, so viel Luft zwischen dem Gelächter einzusparen, daß er nun diese Schreie in die Luft wiehern konnte.

«Schischyphusch!» schrie er und patschte sich gegen die nasse Stirn. «Schischyphusch! Schiiischyyyphuuusch!» Er hielt sich mit beiden Händen an der Tischplatte fest und wieherte: «Schischyphusch!» Als er fast zwei Dutzend mal gewiehert hatte, dieses «Schischyphusch» aus voller Kehle gewiehert hatte, wurde meinem Onkel das Schischyphuschen zuviel. Er zerknitterte dem unaufhörlich wiehernden Kellner mit einem einzigen Griff das gestärkte Hemd, schlug mit der anderen Faust auf den Tisch, daß zwölf leere Gläser an zu springen fingen, und donnerte ihn an: «Schlusch! Schlusch, schag ich jetscht. Wasch scholl dasch mit dieschem blödschinnigen schaudummen Schischyphusch? Schlusch jetscht, verschtehscht du!»

Der Griff und der gedonnerte Baß meines Onkels machten aus dem schischyphuschschreienden Ziegenbock im selben Augenblick wieder den kleinen lispelnden armseligen Kellner.

Er stand auf. Er stand auf, als ob es der größte Irrtum seines Lebens gewesen wäre, daß er sich hingesetzt hatte. Er fuhr sich mit dem Serviettentuch durch das Gesicht und räumte Lachtränen, Schweißtropfen, Asbach und Gelächter wie etwas hinweg, das fluchwürdig und frevelhaft war. Er war aber so betrunken, daß er alles für einen Traum hielt, die Pöbelei am Anfang, das Mitleid und die Freundschaft meines Onkels. Er wußte nicht: Hab ich nun eben Schischy-

a few minutes as though pent up, just now, in between the salvoes of laughter that sparkled from his round mouth like metallic machine-gun fire, he succeeded in ejecting short shrill shrieks. He managed to retain so much breath between the laughs that he could now whinny these cries into the air.

'Thithyphuth!' he cried and slapped his damp brow. 'Thithyphuth! Thiiithyyyphuuuth!' He took a firm hold of the table-top with both hands and neighed: 'Thithyphuth!' After he had neighed about a couple of dozen times, had neighed this 'Thithyphuth' exultantly, the 'thithyphuths' became too much for my uncle. He crumpled the starched shirt of the ceaselessly neighing waiter in one single grip, hammered the other fist on the table so that twelve empty glasses began to dance, and thundered at him: 'Thtop! Thtop it, I thay. What'th thith thilly thtupid Thithyphuth mean? Thtop it now, do you underthtand!'

The grip and my uncle's thundering bass turned the thithyphuth-crying he-goat into the tiny lisping wretched waiter again in one and the same moment.

He stood up. He stood up as if it had been the greatest mistake of his life to have sat down. He brushed his napkin over his face and cleared away tears of laughter, beads of perspiration, brandy, and hilarity like things of the past that were accursed and wanton. But he was so drunk that he took it all for a dream – the familiarity at the outset, the suffering, and the friendship of my uncle. He was in doubt: have I just cried 'Thithyphuth'? Or not? Have I knocked back thix brandieth, I, the waiter

phusch geschrien? Oder nicht? Hab ich schechsch Aschbach gekippt, ich, der Kellner dieschesch Lokalsch, mitten unter den Gäschten? Ich? Er war unsicher. Und für alle Fälle machte er eine abgehackte kleine Verbeugung und flüsterte: «Verscheihung!» Und dann verbeugte er sich noch einmal: «Verscheihung. Ja, verscheihen Schie dasch Schischyphuschgeschrei. Bitte schehr. Verscheihen der Herr, wenn ich schu laut war, aber der Aschbach, Schie wischen ja schelbscht, wenn man nichtsch gegeschen hat, auf leeren Magen. Bitte schehr darum. Schischyphusch war nämlich mein Schpitschname. Ja, in der Schule schon. Die gansche Klasche nannte mich scho. Schie wischen wohl, Schischyphusch, dasch war der Mann in der Hölle, diesche alte Schage, wischen Schie, der Mann im Hadesch, der arme Schünder, der einen groschen Felschen auf einen rieschigen Berg raufschieben schollte, eh, muschte, ja, dasch war der Schischyphusch, wischen Schie wohl. In der Schule muschte ich dasch immer schagen, immer diesch Schischyphusch. Und allesch hat dann gepuschtet vor Lachen, können Schie schich denken, werter Herr. Allesch hat dann gelacht, wischen Schie, schintemalen ich doch die schu kursche Schungenschpitsche beschitsche. Scho kam esch, dasch ich schpäter überall Schischyphusch geheischen wurde und gehänschelt wurde, schehen Schie. Und dasch, verscheihen, kam mir beim Aschbach nun scho insch Gedächtnisch, alsch ich scho geschrien habe, verschtehen. Verscheihen Schie, ich bitte schehr, verscheihen Schie, wenn ich Schie beläschtigt haben schollte, bitte schehr.»

Er verstummte. Seine Serviette war indessen unzählige Male von einer Hand in die andere gewandert. Dann sah er auf meinen Onkel.

Jetzt war der es, der still am Tisch saß und vor sich auf die Tischdecke sah. Er wagte nicht, den Kellner anzusehen. Mein Onkel, mein bärischer bulliger riesiger Onkel wagte

of thith pub, in the middle of my cuthtomerth? Me? He
was not sure. And in any case he made a little truncated
bow and whispered 'Thorry!' And then he bowed
again: 'Thorry. Yeth, pleath forgive the "Thithyphuth" cry. If you pleath. Would the gentleman pleath
forgive me if I wath too loud, but the brandieth, ath you
mutht know yourthelf, if you haven't eaten anything,
on an empty thtomach. Tho pleath. "Thithyphuth" was
actually my nickname. Yeth, at thcool. The whole
clath called me that. You mutht know that Thithyphuth
wath the man in hell, thith old myth, you know, of the
man in Hadeth, the poor thinner, who was thuppothed
to puth a great thtone up a huge mountain, ah, had to,
yeth, that wath Thithyphuth, ath you know. I alwayth
had to tell thith in thcool, alwayth thith Thithyphuth.
And they all burtht with laughter then, ath you may
well imagine, my good thir. They all laughed, you
know, thinthe I had the tip of my tongue too thort. Tho
it came about that later on I wath called Thithyphuth
everywhere and wath teathed, you thee. And that,
thorry, thprang tho much into my mind with the
brandieth, when I thouted out tho, you underthtand.
Forgive me, pleath, forgive me if I have bothered you,
pleath.'

He fell silent. His napkin in the meanwhile had passed
from one hand to the other countless times. Then he
looked at my uncle.

Now it was his turn to sit still at the table and look
down at the table-cloth. He dare not look at the waiter.
My uncle, my bearish, bullish giant uncle dare not raise
his eyes and counter the look of this little self-conscious

nicht, aufzusehen und den Blick dieses kleinen verlegenen Kellners zu erwidern. Und die beiden dicken Tränen, die saßen nun in seinen Augen. Aber das sah keiner außer mir. Und ich sah es auch nur, weil ich so klein war, daß ich ihm von unten her ins Gesicht sehen konnte. Er schob dem still abwartenden Kellner einen mächtigen Geldschein hin, winkte ungeduldig ab, als der ihm zurückgeben wollte, und stand auf, ohne jemanden anzusehen.

Der Kellner brachte noch zaghaft einen Satz an: «Die Aschbach wollte ich wohl gern beschahlt haben, bitte schehr.»

Dabei hatte er den Schein schon in seine Tasche gesteckt, als erwarte er keine Antwort und keinen Einspruch. Es hatte auch keiner den Satz gehört und seine Großzügigkeit fiel lautlos auf den harten Kies des Gartenlokals und wurde da später gleichgültig zertreten. Mein Onkel nahm seinen Stock, wir standen auf, meine Mutter stützte meinen Onkel und wir gingen langsam auf die Straße zu. Keiner von uns dreien sah auf den Kellner. Meine Mutter und ich nicht, weil wir uns schämten. Mein Onkel nicht, weil er die beiden Tränen in den Augen sitzen hatte. Vielleicht schämte er sich auch, dieser Onkel. Langsam kamen wir auf den Ausgang zu, der Stock meines Onkels knirschte häßlich auf dem Gartenkies und das war das einzige Geräusch im Augenblick, denn die drei bis vierhundert Gesichter an den Tischen waren stumm und glotzäugig auf unseren Abgang konzentriert.

Und plötzlich tat mir der kleine Kellner leid. Als wir am Ausgang des Gartens um die Ecke biegen wollten, sah ich mich schnell noch einmal nach ihm um. Er stand noch immer an unserem Tisch. Sein weißes Serviettentuch hing bis auf die Erde. Er schien mir noch viel viel kleiner geworden zu sein. So klein stand er da und ich liebte ihn plötzlich, als ich ihn so verlassen hinter uns herblicken sah,

waiter. And the two full tears that now welled in his eyes. But no one except me saw that. And I only saw it because I was so small that I could look up into his face from below. He pushed an extravagant banknote over to the motionless, expectant waiter, impatiently waved him off when he wanted to give it back, and stood up without looking at anyone.

The waiter, timid still, produced another sentence: 'The brandieth I would have liked to have paid for my-thelf, if you pleath.'

However, he had already put the note in his wallet, as though he expected no answer and no protest. Moreover, no one had heard the sentence and his generosity fell silently on the hard gravel of the beer-garden and was there later trampled indifferently underfoot. My uncle took his stick, we stood up, my mother supported my uncle and we went slowly out to the street. None of us three looked at the waiter. Not my mother and I, because we were ashamed. Not my uncle, for he had those two tears in his eyes. Perhaps he was ashamed too, this uncle. Slowly we approached the exit; my uncle's stick crunched nastily in the garden gravel, and this was the only sound for the moment, for the three to four hundred faces at the tables were concentrated, mute and goggle-eyed, on our departure.

And suddenly I felt sorry for the little waiter. As we were about to turn the corner at the beer-garden exit, I looked quickly round at him once again. He was still standing at our table. His white napkin hung down to the ground. He seemed to me to have become much, much smaller. He stood there so small, and I loved him suddenly when I saw him stare our way, so forsaken behind us, so small, so grey, so empty, so poor, so cold,

so klein, so grau, so leer, so hoffnungslos, so arm, so kalt und so grenzenlos allein! Ach, wie klein! Er tat mir so unendlich leid, daß ich meinen Onkel an die Hand tippte, aufgeregt, und leise sagte: «Ich glaube, jetzt weint er.»

Mein Onkel blieb stehen. Er sah mich an und ich konnte die beiden dicken Tropfen in seinen Augen ganz deutlich erkennen. Noch einmal sagte ich, ohne genau zu verstehen, warum ich es eigentlich tat: «Oh, er weint. Kuck mal,[13] er weint.»

Da ließ mein Onkel den Arm meiner Mutter los, humpelte schnell und schwer zwei Schritte zurück, riß seinen Krückstock wie ein Schwert hoch und stach damit in den Himmel und brüllte mit der ganzen großartigen Kraft seines gewaltigen Körpers und seiner Kehle:

«Schischyphusch! Schischyphusch! Hörscht du? Auf Wiederschehen, alter Schischyphusch! Bisch nächschten Schonntag, dummesch Luder! Wiederschehen!»

Die beiden dicken Tränen wurden von den Falten, die sich jetzt über sein gutes braunes Gesicht zogen, zu nichts zerdrückt. Es waren Lachfalten und er hatte das ganze Gesicht voll davon. Noch einmal fegte er mit seinem Krückstock über den Himmel, als wollte er die Sonne herunterraken, und noch einmal donnerte er sein Riesenlachen über die Tische des Gartenlokals hin: «Schischyphusch! Schsichyphusch!»

Und Schischyphusch, der kleine graue arme Kellner, wachte aus seinem Tod auf, hob seine Serviette und fuhr damit auf und ab wie ein wildgewordener Fensterputzer. Er wischte die ganze graue Welt, alle Gartenlokale der Welt, alle Kellner und alle Zungenfehler der Welt mit seinem Winken endgültig und für immer weg aus seinem Leben. Und er schrie schrill und überglücklich zurück, wobei er sich auf die Zehen stellte, und ohne sein Fensterputzen zu unterbrechen:

and so immensely alone! Oh, how small! He gave me such infinite pain that I was moved to tap my uncle's hand, and I said quietly: 'I think he is crying now.'

My uncle stopped. He looked at me and I could make out the two full tears in his eyes quite clearly. I said yet again, without fully understanding why I really did it: 'Oh, he's crying. Just look, he's crying.'

Then my uncle let go of my mother's arm, hobbled a couple of swift, solid steps back, heaved his crutch high like a sword and stabbed into the sky with it and bellowed with the whole grand power of his mighty body and his lungs:

'Thithyphuth! Thithyphuth! Can you hear? *Au revoir*, old Thithyphuth! Till nextht Thunday, poor beatht! Wiederthehen!'

The two full tears were crushed to nothing by the wrinkles that now spread over his good brown features. They were creases of laughter and his whole face was full of them. Once again he swept the skies with his crutch, as if he wanted to rake down the sun, and again his giant laughter thundered away over the beer-garden tables: 'Thithyphuth! Thithyphuth!'

And Thithyphuth, the poor little grey waiter, awoke from the dead, raised his napkin and worked it up and down like a window-cleaner gone beserk. He wiped away the whole grey world, all the beer-gardens of the world, all waiters, and all the speech-defects of the world with his waving, finally and for ever out of his life. And he shouted back, shrill and overjoyed, standing on tiptoe, without interrupting his window-cleaning:

«Ich verschtehe! Bitte schehr! Am Schonntag! Ja, Wiederschehen! Am Schonntag, bitte schehr!»

Dann bogen wir um die Ecke. Mein Onkel griff wieder nach dem Arm meiner Mutter und sagte leise: «Ich weisch, esch war schicher entschetschlich für euch. Aber wasch schollte ich andersch tun, schag schelbscht. Scho'n dummer Hasche. Läuft nun schein gansches Leben mit scho einem garschtigen Schungenfehler herum. Armesch Luder dasch!»

'I underthtand! Yeth pleath! On Thunday! Yeth, *au revoir*! On Thunday, pleath!'

Then we turned the corner. My uncle **caught** hold of my mother's arm again and said softly: '**I know** it wath quite dreadful for you. But what elthe **could** I do, tell me that? Thuch a thilly donkey. Running around all hith life with a nathty thpeech impediment like that. Poor beatht!'

NOTES ON GERMAN TEXTS

PALE ANNA (*Böll*)

1. The two English verbs seem to render '*döste vor mich hin*' more precisely than one (e.g. 'vegetated').
2. '*Voller*': literally , 'full of', but can be used fairly freely, e.g. '*voller Papier liegen*', to be littered with paper.
3. This would be the usual mock-up background used by certain photographers at the time for pictures of soldiers. '*Reben*' is used in a limited sense for 'vines', in a general sense for 'creepers' (also *Ranken*).
4. The numbers indicate the group's 'year' in school.
5. This passage might be rendered: 'Only when I'd been there and had taken ....' '*Wohnte*', because the action was still in progress; '*hatte*' is understood after '*genommen*'.
6. Literally: 'broken into crumbs'; '*der Brosame*' (also '*die Brosame*'): crumb (also '*der Brocken*'), but is more commonly used only in the plural: '*Brosamen*'.
7. '*Dabei*' has the sense of 'at it' or 'in it' ('present at' or 'in'). '*Ich war dabei*' is the colloquial equivalent of English quasi-heroic 'I was there' (meaning present in some military action). The narrator's use of the term in the next sentence is, naturally, ironic.

STORY IN REVERSE (*Aichinger*)

1. Literally: 'a minor'. Here a carefree, *young* child is implied.
2. In addressing the public, official notices vary between second and third person plural.
3. Strictly, '*denn*' is used to give the logical reason, the reason being one that can be easily verified, whereas *weil* and *da* give the real or moral reason, e.g. *Es muß kalt draußen sein, denn der Teich ist zugefroren* but *Der Teich ist zugefroren, weil es so kalt ist* (cf. H. F. Eggeling, *A Dictionary of Modern German Prose Usage*, Oxford, 1951).

4. '*Dafür wird man heute noch verbrannt*': this is the only point in the story where the narrator returns momentarily to objective reality, the viewpoint being elsewhere entirely subjective.

5. '*Zu jubeln begonnen*': this contains also the sense of 'to quicken'.

6. See note 5 above.

7. Literally: 'the coal mountains'.

8. Literally: 'everything seeks its time'.

9. '*Die über die Mauern hängen*': normally one would expect the dative here after 'über', since position rather than movement is indicated, but this would not imply the stretching of the twigs, the suggestion of reaching across, that is here needed.

10. '*Du bringst sie zur Ruhe*': this also has the meaning of 'to put to bed'.

THE HOST (*Bender*)

1. *Taxieren*: 'to guess, to surmise the value of something.'

2. '*Dämchen*': this diminutive is used (1) merely ironically i.e. 'the little lady'; (2) for a dolled-up woman; (3) as an equivalent of 'lady of easy virtue'.

3. Cider tavern is the literal and not very satisfactory rendering of '*Obstweingaststätte*'. The 'fruit wine' sold in such places is in fact a potent alcoholic drink comparable with vintage cider.

4. '*Kiosk*': a little hut where newspapers or refreshments are sold.

5. *Streunen, ich streune, (habe gestreunt)*: 'roaming, loafing about'. *Der Streuner*: 'the vagabond'.

6. *Den Rahm abschöpfen*: 'taking off the cream'. Also used in a figurative sense.

7. '*Freie Zeche*': literally 'free of charge'; *ich zeche*: 'I drink, booze, carouse'. Idiomatically, *Er muß die Zeche bezahlen*: 'he has to pay the bill, face the music'; *Der Zechenbruder*: 'boon companion'. It is not unusual in popular German dance halls to employ *Animierherren* as well as *Animiermädchen* whose job it is to partner single customers.

8. '*Schuft*': literally, 'rascal, blackguard'.

9. '*Kneipe*': 'a low public-house, a tavern, beer joint, dive'.

10. The following passage describes, with the use of the imperfect tense, a habitual action, rather than the single action

of the narrative. On this particular evening 'Lohengrin' is merely described as being there, not as being drunk.

11. *Das Rondell*: an English equivalent would be, for example, the centre island with Bush House in the Strand, London.

12. '*Querstraße*': literally the road that crosses the road you are in. 'Cross-road' would be rendered by *Kreuzung*.

WOMAN DRIVER (*Fussenegger*)

1. '*Sauber*': a fashionable word, here: 'well, carefully'; cf. '*clean* licence (record)'.

2. '*Daheim*': South German for *zu Hause* (cf. p. 84, l. 17, where *heimfahren* = *nach Hause fahren*).

3. *Glosen*: South German for '*glühen*', 'to glow, gleam'.

4. '*Das Geschoß*': 'projectile, missile' – a reference to the first successful Russian moon-shot.

5. *Anschweigen*: an unusual verb, meaning 'to address oneself silently to, address one's silence to' (cf. *anreden*), hence 'to address a silent appeal/reproach/challenge/invitation to'.

6. *Das Eck*, South German for *die Ecke*.

7. *Zerblättern*: unusual figurative usage; the verb is usually transitive, meaning 'to strip of leaves'. In this context the reflexive *sich zerblättern* would be expected.

8. *Spinnen*: (1) 'to follow the thread of a thought', (2) 'to spin' (a web), (3) 'to be crazy'; here all three meanings are present.

9. '*Zu Wagen*': by analogy with '*zu Pferd*'.

10. '*Spulen*': normally transitive, 'to reel, spool' (cf. *spülen*, intransitive, meaning 'to wash (against)').

11. *Entwesen* = '*verwesen*': 'to dissolve, lose essence, become insubstantial and turn into'. A phrase such as '*alle Dinge entwest*', with plural subject and singular verb, is normally not found in written German, although in Middle High German a singular verb was frequently found with a compound or collective subject, and even with a plural one; medieval writers, perceiving 'unity in diversity', sometimes saw the subject (despite its grammatical form) as one 'idea', and therefore used a singular verb. Here '*Alle Dinge*' = *alles*, hence the unusual (Austrian dialect) form which is peculiarly appropriate.

ANTIGONE AND THE GARDEN DWARF (*Gaiser*)

1. *Dämon* cannot adequately be translated by the English word 'demon', nor by any other. As well as its normal meaning, it carries overtones given to it by the *Sturm und Drang* writers of the eighteenth century, particularly Goethe. It was used then, like the Greek '*daimon*', to mean the genius, or obsession, driving the dynamic, creative man. In this story *Dämon* is not used primarily in this sense, but these overtones should not be forgotten.

2. Moritz von Schwind (1804–71), Romantic painter, famous for his illustrations, mainly in water-colour, of German fairy-tales and legends.

3. Whether by chance or by intention, this dream conveys the nightmare frenzy of Hitler addressing a Nazi meeting.

4. Silvia's story is in the historic present, here given in the past because a long narration in the historic present is as uncommon a device in English as it is common in German.

5. *Jähzornig*: literally, 'irascible, hot-tempered'.

6. '*Eines*', used in the sense of 'chap, body', is not a contraction but a deliberate lapse into grammatical error which reflects both the skin-deep refinement and the obsessive haste of Silvia's customer.

7. *Fuchteln*: literally, to brandish or fidget with a sword or rod (*Fuchtel*). *Fisteln*: to sing falsetto. The two words together have the single meaning: to gesticulate – just as 'he huffed and he puffed' would have to be rendered in German by a single word.

8. *Gleichgültig bleiben*: literally, 'remain indifferent'.

9. '*Suppengrün*': mixed herbs, usually chives and parsley, which are chopped and scattered on to soup when served.

10. The original is precisely as ambiguous as the translation. It is impossible to say whether the woman in the garden is the man's wife or not; whether she is at death's door or not; or indeed whether any woman at all has been at death's door. What is clear, however, is that it is our apoplectic friend and not his wife (if she exists) who is obsessed with garden dwarfs.

11. '*Vitzliputz*': abbreviation for '*Vitzliputzli*', a corruption of the name of one of the Aztecs' principal gods. Huitzilo-pochtli, the Humming-bird Wizard, War God, and Sun

God, was the chief god of Tenochtitlan (the present Mexico City) where he had a huge temple.

12. *'Nimmt er uns an'*: here, literally, 'he closes with us'.

13. *'Meckernd'*: the allusion is presumably to the goat's body, which the devil is sometimes said to take.

14. *'Wie ist das mit dem Geld geworden'*: literally, 'how did it turn out about the money'.

15. *Taugen*: literally, 'to be good/fit for'.

AT THE TROCADERO (*Schnurre*)

1. *'Flöten gegangen'* is a slang expression comparable to 'gone for a Burton'.

2. *Die Kluft*: slang of Jewish origin, for 'dress, suit'.

3. *Die Pantine*: 'patten', a heavy shoe with wooden sole and leather or thong top.

4. Deutsch Krone, Schneidemühl: from 1922 to 1938 in the border march of Posen, West Prussia; from 1938 in the province of Pomerania (now part of Poland).

5. *Hecheln*: literally, 'to hackle, comb, tease' (of flax).

6. *Grienen*: form of *grinsen*, 'to grin'.

7. *Stülpen*: 'to slap, jam' (e.g. of hat on head).

8. *Die Dohle*: literally, 'jackdaw'; slang for 'disreputable woman'.

9. *Die Schlenke*: literally, 'gully'.

10. *'Binsenkubben'* = *die Binse*: 'rush, sedge'; *die Kubbe*: Frisian for 'gull'.

11. *'Tja, denn'*: emotive particles, a common feature of spoken German.

12. Literally, 'clink glasses with me', the equivalent of 'Cheers!' (*Prost!*).

WHEN POTEMKIN'S COACH WENT BY (*Lettau*)

1. When the second of two statements is made, as it is here, in the word order of a question, and *doch* is inserted, the force of *doch* is causal.

2. *Stoßen auf* (*etwas*) is often used in the literal sense 'to strike' as of a ship hitting rocks. Here, it is used in a comparatively common metaphorical sense 'to come across'.

3. *Väterchen* is the diminutive affectionate form of *Vater*. The literal translation of *Aufseher* is 'foreman' or 'oldish man'.
4. Literally, 'chimney builders'. Where houses were built of wood, theirs would presumably be a special craft.
5. The subjunctive is here used, as though in reported speech or thought, because the events are those of a dream and are therefore regarded as contingent.
6. Prince Grigory Aleksandrovich Potemkin, who lived from 1739 to 1791, was one of the many favourites of Catherine II of Russia, and rose to high office in her administration as commander-in-chief and governor-general of 'New Russia': the conquered provinces of the Ukraine. He conducted the journey to the south which Catherine made in 1787. It is suggested that he had sham villages built in preparation for her visit in order to please and impress her. According to a more probable version of the tale, he confined his deception to concealing the fact that towns for which she had provided large sums of money had not been completed.
7. '*Kam . . . gelaufen*': 'came running'. It is normal for German to use the past participle, where English would use the present, in conjunction with the past tense of a verb of motion. This usage is also increasingly common in modern German with verbs of sound.
8. The verb *erwählen* is used in modern German with the accusative for the person, and *zu* plus the dative case for the office to which he is elected, as in *Sie erwählten ihn zum König*. Here the noun follows the same pattern.
9. Meaning: 'in an hour's time'. *Frist* means 'a period of time', and 'respite' or 'delay'. In this compound, it clearly has the second sense.

THITHYPHUTH (*Borchert*)

1. Normally used in a pejorative sense: to hound, shadow, etc., an enemy.
2. Not a true lisp, as is apparent in the story, but with the effect in German of 'sch' for 's' and 'z'; the transliteration 'th' has been adopted in the translation.
3. i.e. Asbach Uralt, the name of a brand made by the firm Asbach.

4. i.e. sick with anger; not in best usage.

5. Literally, 'bee-sting'. A cake covered with chopped almonds and coconut, butter, honey, etc., made in a pastry mould.

6. Unnaturally; literally, like a raven's mother; the raven sometimes ejects its young from the nest.

7. Literally, 'territory', 'precinct'. Here, the area of tables allocated to and served exclusively by one waiter.

8. Meaning both parable and parabola, in the geometric sense; here, the equivalent of *Wurflinie*, a projectile line, or trajectory, of a missile.

9. Actually a term of obscene abuse.

10. These verbs are typical onomatopoeic inventions of the author.

11. The adjective from Vierlande, a suburb of Hamburg whose fertile lowland has made market-gardening its speciality.

12. = *Felsenquelle*, a mountain spring, etc.

13. Familiar usage.

refresh yourself at penguin.co.uk

Visit penguin.co.uk for exclusive information and interviews with
bestselling authors, fantastic give-aways and the
inside track on all our books, from the Penguin Classics
to the latest bestsellers.

BE FIRST ▼

first chapters, first editions, first novels

EXCLUSIVES ▼

author chats, video interviews, biographies, special
features

EVERYONE'S A WINNER ▼

give-aways, competitions, quizzes, ecards

READERS GROUPS ▼

exciting features to support existing groups and
create new ones

NEWS ▼

author events, bestsellers, awards, what's new

EBOOKS ▼

books that click – download an ePenguin today

BROWSE AND BUY ▼

thousands of books to investigate – search, try
and buy the perfect gift online – or treat yourself!

ABOUT US ▼

job vacancies, advice for writers and company
history

Get Closer To Penguin . . . www.penguin.co.uk